ABOUT
HAIGH & ASPULL

by
M. D. Smith

This Book is dedicated to the Memory of John and Dorothy Pendlebury
of Higher Highfield Farm, Aspull

John and Dorothy Pendlebury
circa 1951.

Wyre Publishing
c/o David Smith, 27 Sutton Lane, Adlington, Lancashire PR6 9PA

Wigan Taxi Bus Service on Haigh Road, near the Balcarres Arms, 1925.

Mr T. Sefton of the Running Horses Hotel, Aspull, ran this service between Haigh and Wigan. Taxi Bus fares ranged from 5d. from Haigh to Wigan with 1d. charged from Haigh to the Finger Post. Buses ran hourly from 8.20am until 10.40pm between Wigan and Haigh and between 8.00am and 9.50pm from Haigh Church to Wigan. A Sunday service was also provided.

TABLE OF CONTENTS

A joint procession was organised through Haigh and Aspull to celebrate the Coronation of George V and Queen Mary. Children rode through the streets on gaily decorated lorries. Each child was supplied with refreshments and given a newly minted penny bearing the new King's head. The lorry shown is parked on the Windmill Field.

ABOUT HAIGH AND ASPULL

INTRODUCTION

It was originally my intention to write about Haigh as a natural geographical progression of my earlier works on Adlington and Blackrod.

The boundary between Haigh and Aspull runs along Haigh Road, past St. David's Church, and then follows a devious course through the Plantations to Wigan Road, New Springs. There are actually properties in Haigh Road which are divided by the boundary line, so that in one part of the house you are in Haigh, while in another part you are in Aspull. It has therefore proved inappropriate to deal with Haigh in isolation. Both Haigh and Aspull are inextricably linked and it has been necessary to include reference to both in order to strike a reasonable balance. This has increased the work involved but has proved doubly rewarding.

There is so much of interest to write about, that the hardest decisions have centred on what to omit, rather than the actual contents. Fortunately, a number of publications already exist concerning Haigh Hall, the local collieries, and railways in the district. The content of these works has been taken account of when formulating the structure of the project .Any work on local history forges a link in an endless chain and leaves plenty of opportunity for further addition. However, the link must be of sufficient strength in terms of interest and understanding to be of value.

Without help, the task of compiling a book such as this is a daunting prospect, however, even a handful of interested people can lighten the burden and expedite matters. I have been very fortunate in receiving assistance from a wide variety of people, whose names are included in the acknowledgement section. It is to them that the greater credit is due. Any mistakes I must claim for myself.

It is always an enjoyable enterprise to find out about neighbouring towns and villages and document the findings. I sincerely hope that this book proves as interesting to the reader as the pleasure it has given me to be involved in its compilation.

Malcolm David Smith
Adlington, Lancashire
December 2000.

ABOUT HAIGH

"The venerable house of Haigh is closely connected with the history of Wigan, and is geographically so situated on the rising ground in the east of the town, as if meant to oversee all its acts and take a guardian interest in burghal progress. Whilst the hall is itself sheltered from the bitter east winds, it commands a pleasant view of the undulating western plain in which the old borough is situated. It is said that in very clear weather the Isle of Man can be seen from it. On the same site was the home of the Bradshaighs, and within two miles of it the abode of the Norrys, the last of whose direct race was Mabella. The honourable family now inhabiting it have been ornaments to their town and country. They have been distinguished in war, politics, religion, literature and science. Thence have come many of the most distinguished mayors and parliamentary representatives of the borough.

The hall of the Norrys, within four miles of Wigan, with the houses of the retainers, was anciently the nucleus of a small but according to the beliefs of many, an important town called Blackrod".

The History of Wigan by David Sinclair (1882).

NORRIS ARMS.

Early 19th Century engraving of Haigh Hall showing the observatory on the right.
The Armorial bearings of the Norris and Bradshaigh families can also be seen in this picture

ORIGIN OF THE NAME 'HAIGH'

According to the 'Concise Oxford Dictionary of English Place Names' by Eilert Ekwall, the name 'Haigh' is derived from either the old English word 'haga' which means fence or fenced enclosure or the Old Scandinavian word 'hagi' meaning enclosure. References are made to 'Hage' in the Lancashire Pipe Rolls for 1194 and 'Hagh' in the Feet of Fines for the County of Lancaster in 1298.

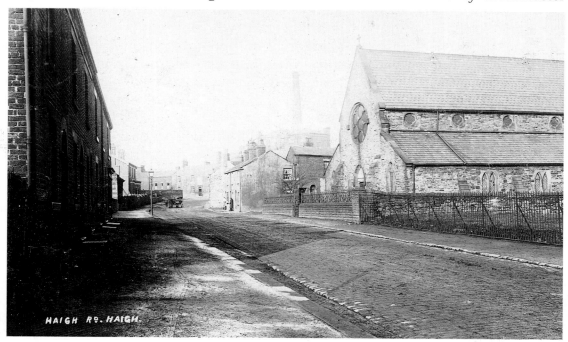

Haigh Road 1904
The church on the right is Our Lady of the Immaculate Conception, R.C. Church; built in 1857-58 by J.Goodwin.
Haigh Brewery chimney can be seen in the centre.

Haigh House, Haigh 1908.

A game of bowls is in progress on the fields off Haigh Road, Haigh (Circa 1900)
Butcherfield Row can be seen in the background

THE MANOR OF HAIGH

When Lancashire was divided into 'Hundreds', Haigh was one of the townships of Wigan, situated in the hundred of West Derby. `Baines' History of Lancashire` contains the following passage:-

"HAIGH. - The most interesting amongst the numerous townships of Wigan is Haigh, a well-cultivated and populous district, stored with mines of coal and cannel, and rich in iron ore. There is here a large iron foundry, the property of the earl of Crawford and Balcarres, who resides at the stately mansion of Haigh Hall, having succeeded to the estates on the death of his father on the 25th March 1825. In 1826, James Lindsay, earl of Balcarres, and Lord Lindsay, county Fife, was created a peer of the United Kingdom, by the title of Baron Wigan, of Haigh Hall, county Lancashire".

The Manor of Haigh was originally owned by the Norris family, referred to in Latin records as Norrenses, and in Norman-French records as le Norreis, or le Norreys. They were also lords of Sutton, Rainhill, Whiston, Blackrode (Blackrod) and Westley (West Leigh). Haigh and Blackrod were held as a twelfth part of a knight's fee, and paid for accordingly.

In either 1199 or 1200, during the reign of King John, Hugh le Norreis obtained a charter for Blackrod, and in 1201-2 he paid to the king, two marks and two chascurs (hunters) for a confirmation of his title.

Another Hugh Norreys, who held the manors of Haigh and Blackrod, had a daughter and co-heiress, Mabilla, who married Sir William Bradshaigh, and thus conveyed the manor into this family. They made Haigh Hall their principal residence until the death of the last baronet of that name.

It was in about 1295 that Sir William Bradshaigh and Mabel (Mabilla) Norreys were married and it is this couple who are associated with the legend of Mab's Cross. There are several versions of the legend but the basic facts are as follows:-

During the early fourteenth century Sir William Bradshaigh was involved in either events after the Battle of Bannockburn in 1314, or the Banastre Rebellion of 1315; following which he was forced to flee abroad for his life. He was absent for some seven years during which time his wife Mabel was informed of his death by either Osmond Neville, a Welsh Knight, or Sir Henry Teuther. The upshot was that Mabel subsequently married the informant.

After a period of approximately seven years, Sir William Bradshaigh returned from exile. One story is that he went to Haigh dressed in a palmer's habit and mixed amongst the poor. (In Medieval Europe a palmer was a pilgrim bearing a palm branch as a sign of his visit to the Holy Land.). However, John Roby, in his book 'Traditions of Lancashire' has shown that Sir William Bradshaigh was not involved in the Holy Wars, having only been born some years after they had finished. On seeing the pilgrim and how much he resembled her deceased husband, Mabel wept and was chastised by her, then, husband. Sir William Bradshaigh made himself known and Mabel's bigamous spouse fled. He was pursued by Sir William who eventually caught up with him at Newton-le-Willows where he was put to death.

As punishment, Dame Mabel was enjoined by her priest confessor to do penance by going once a week, barefoot and bare-legged, to a cross near Wigan, from her home at Haigh. Sir William Bradshaigh was reportedly killed by the relatives of Sir Henry de Bury in 1333. He was slain in Newton-le-Willows close to the spot where he is said to have killed the Welsh Knight

An early engraving of Mab's Cross, Wigan, from a drawing by G. Pickering.

Standishgate, Wigan, 1904.

On the 6th October 1919 Mab's Cross was removed from its ancient site during the street widening of Standishgate.

Standishgate, Wigan, circa 1935.

On the 23rd August 1921 Mab's Cross was re-erected in the grounds of the Wigan Girls' High School.

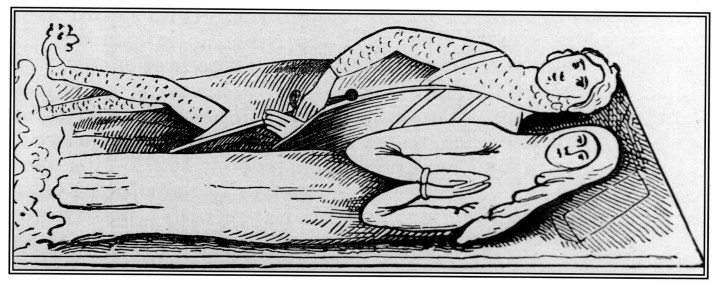

In 1664, Sir William Dugdale sketched the tomb of Sir William Bradshaigh and Dame Mabel.
The drawing above is a facsimile of the original included in Baines History of Lancashire.

Dame Mabel founded chantry chapels in the Parish Church of Wigan and Blackrod Chapel. The former was dedicated to St. Mary the Virgin and the latter to St. Katherine the Virgin. There is some confusion as to when the chantries were actually established. Blackrod Parish Registers indicate that the Blackrod Chantry was founded shortly before the 8th June 1335, while Sinclair's History of Wigan contains the following reference:-

"The lady Mabella survived her husband, Sir William Bradshaigh, and founded a chantry in the Chapel of Blackrod in 1338, which she dedicated to St. Katherine the Virgin, giving as an endowment two messuages, sixty acres of land, eight acres of meadow, ten acres of wood, with their appurtenances, in Blackrode, with turbary of the said messuages, to have and to hold to the chantry priest and his successors for ever, saying divine service daily in the said Chapel of Blackrode for ever, making special mention of the name of Mabella in mass celebrations".

In the previous year, 1337, Dame Mabella is recorded by Sinclair as founding the chantry in Wigan Parish Church.

Sir William Bradshaigh was buried in the chapel at Wigan Parish Church during 1333 and following her death, in 1348, Lady Mabel was laid to rest beside her husband. An altar tomb was erected to their memory with money left for the purpose. The effigies of the couple lying beside each other were carved on top. His effigy was in chain-mail, cross-legged, with his sword partially drawn from the scabbard on his left side, with a shield charged with two bends, the Bradshaigh arms; hers in a long robe, veiled, her hands elevated and joined over her breast in an attitude of prayer.

MANOR
OF
HAIGH,
In the County of Lancaster,
TO WIT.

By VIRTUE of a Precept under the Hand and Seal of ROGER GRIMSHAW, Gentleman, Steward of the said Manor, I do hereby summon and require all Persons who owe Suit and Service at the Court Leet, View of Frank Pledge, and Court Baron, of THE RIGHT HONORABLE *ALEXANDER EARL OF BALCARRES*, LORD OF THE SAID MANOR, to be and appear at the Court Leet, View of Frank Pledge, and Court Baron of the said EARL, to be held at the House of JAMES WALLS, the Sign of the *Packet Boat*, within the said Manor, on *Monday the Seventh Day of September next*, at the Hour of *Nine in the Forenoon* of the same Day; when and where the said Court will be held; and afterwards the Boundaries of the said Manor perambulated.—Dated this   Day of August, 1818.

Bailiff of the said Manor.

D. LYON, PRINTER, MARKET-PLACE, WIGAN.

Subsequent to the death of Lady Mabel, Haigh estate was settled on Sir William's nephew, also William de Bradshaigh. Roger de Bradshaigh, Mabel's brother-in-law, inherited the manor of Blackrod.

Haigh estate remained in the Bradshaigh family, passing to male issue, until the death of Sir Roger de Bradshaigh, the fourth baronet, who died without male issue. The estate was then devolved on his great-grandaughter, Elizabeth Bradshaigh Dalrymple, daughter of Charles Dalrymple, Esq., of North Berwick, being the sole heir and representative of the Bradshaigh family.

On the 1st June 1780, this lady married her cousin, Alexander, sixth Earl of Balcarres, for some time Govenor of Jamaica, who succeeded as the twenty-third Earl of Crawford in 1808.

There was an annual custom of walking the boundaries of the manor to determine possession and the interesting notice included was a summons to the residents to attend both the Court Leet and perambulate the boundaries of Haigh Manor.

Alexander, the sixth Earl of Crawford and Balcarres died on the 27th March 1825, and was succeeded by his son

James. He was created Baron Wigan of Haigh Hall by patent dated the 5th July 1826, and received confirmation of the earldom of Crawford in 1848.

Following James's death, on the 15th December 1869, his eldest son, Alexander William Crawford Linsay, became the twenty fifth Earl of Crawford and the eighth Earl of Balcarres. He married his second cousin, Margaret, eldest daughter of Lieutenant General James Lindsay, of Balcarres and the couple had one son, James Ludovic Lindsay. On the death of his father on the 13th December 1880, James Ludovic Lindsay perpetuated the family titles.

Robert Alexander Lindsay was the last of his noble family to inhabit Haigh Hall. He succeeded his father in 1940 as the twenty eighth Earl of Crawford and the eleventh Earl of Balcarres. Other opulent properties were owned in Balcarres, Scotland, and at No. 7 Audley Square, London. The latter property was bombed during the Second World War and subsequently sold. All the contents were transferred to Haigh Hall cellars along with exhibits from various museums.

Payment of death duties forced the sale of 1,616 acres of Haigh Estate in May 1943, and a further 1,027 acres were sold in December 1947. The majority of this land was sold to existing tenants on the estate. (Details from the catalogue of the sale in 1943 are included at Appendix 1).

Reluctantly, the Lindsay family decided to sell Haigh Hall and Park and move to their estate in Scotland. Wigan Corporation purchased the hall and 237 acres for £18,000 in May 1947..
The remaining 124 acres comprising Haigh Park were acquired by Wigan Corporation for £35,000 in 1969.

PARISH CHURCH, WIGAN.

Photograph of the Bradshaigh Tomb in Wigan Parish Church, 1925.

HAIGH HALL

The Lords of Haigh Manor have occupied a residence on the same site for many centuries. A great deal of alteration and re-furbishment has been carried out to the property down the years and complete re-building has been necessary on occasions.

A view of Haigh Hall, as it appeared at the beginning of the eighteenth century, appears in Baines's History of Lancashire and is reproduced below. The grounds were laid out in the Flemish fashion.

On the death of Roger Bradshaigh in 1770, the estate was inherited by his great grand-daughter, Elizabeth Bradshaigh Dalrymple, then only ten years of age. She subsequently married her cousin, Alexander Lindsay, on the 1st June 1780. The Lindsay family held the Earldom of Crawford, the premier Earldom in Scotland.

Haigh Hall had been uninhabited for ten years and was in a bad state of repair, some of which was due to subsidence. Despite severe financial problems, Earl Alexander endeavoured to arrest the decay at Haigh Hall. Buttresses were erected to alleviate the damage caused by subsidence. He also did much to improve the family fortunes.

Alexander Lindsay's eldest son, James was born in 1783. He was M.P. for Wigan from 1820-1825. On the death of his father, on the 27th March, 1825, James succeeded to the estate.

Earl James was a practical man and an engineer. He undertook the task of rebuilding Haigh Hall, on the same site. Some parts of the hall, which were demolished, were extremely old being built of

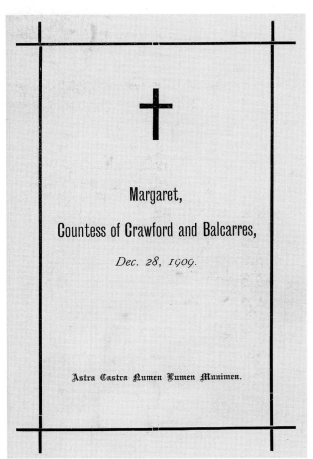

Margaret,
Countess of Crawford and Balcarres,

Dec. 28, 1909.

Astra Castra Numen Lumen Munimen.

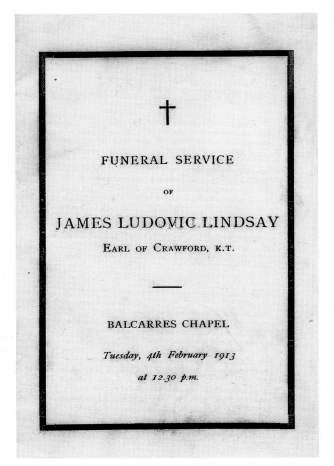

FUNERAL SERVICE

OF

JAMES LUDOVIC LINDSAY

EARL OF CRAWFORD, K.T.

———

BALCARRES CHAPEL

*Tuesday, 4th February 1913
at 12.30 p.m.*

heavy oak baulks. Much of the design for the new hall was inspired by Birchley Hall, Billinge.

Nikolaus Pevsner in 'The Buildings of England-North Lancashire,' comments: - "Haigh Hall. Built 1827-40 for the 24th Earl of Crawford and Balcarres and, it is said, to his own design".

Whilst the work was being carried out at Haigh Hall, Earl James lived in Park Cottage on the estate and earned the nickname 'Jimmy in the Trees'.

Stone was quarried from the Parbold area and transported to the hall by canal where it was dressed on site with specially designed steam-driven saws. Unfortunately the supply was exhausted before completion of the new hall and the original design had to be amended. The result of this was that the walls now lean outwards from the perpendicular.

Materials from the old hall were incorporated into the design and the ironwork used in construction was manufactured at Haigh Foundry.

All the formal ornamental gardens and terracing were replaced by open parkland.

During the Lancashire cotton famine of 1861-3, Earl James gave employment to a great deal of men who were responsible for the construction of 40 miles of pathways running throughout the Haigh estate. Unemployment was rife at the time and the work provided allowed many families to maintain their dignity through this difficult period. The manorial lord engendered much goodwill by his generosity and was an extremely popular figure.

Alexander William Crawford Lindsay, the 25th Earl of Crawford, and 8th Earl of Balcarres (1812-1880) was an avid collector of books and works of art. Together with his son, James Ludovic, he set up at Haigh Hall one of the finest libraries in England.

A much reported event is the visit of the Prince and Princess of Wales (later King Edward the Seventh and Queen Alexandra) to Haigh Hall, in June 1873, when the Royal couple opened the new Royal Albert Edward Infirmary.

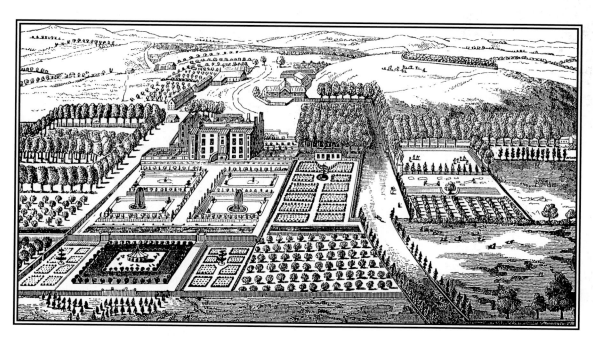

A view of Haigh Hall, as it appeared at the beginning of the eighteeneth century, when the grounds of our English gentry were laid out in the Flemish fashion.

In deference to the Royal visitors, the hall was completely re-decorated re-carpeted and curtained at a cost of £80,000. The boudoir was specially decorated for the Princess in white and gold. Poles were erected along the driveway on which banners were displayed and the whole two miles of the driveway resembled a floral arcade with two triumphal archways decorated with evergreens and banners.

Following their stay at Haigh Hall, the apartments occupied by the Royal visitors were thrown open to the public for three days. The locals were each charged sixpence to view the relevant rooms and the total proceeds were donated to the Royal Albert Edward Infirmary.

Haigh Hall was put to good use during the two World Wars. Casualties were housed there during the 1914-1918 conflict, whilst during the Second World War it was equipped to house any overflow from Wigan Infirmary displaced due to air raids.

In 1947 the hall and grounds were purchased by Wigan Corporation and for some time it was used for exhibitions and wedding receptions, etc.

Mr Frank Penninck was the designer of Haigh Golf Course. He made his first visit to the estate on the 22nd July 1970. Construction work commenced on the 22nd December 1970, and the Mayor of Wigan, Councillor Mrs. Ethel Naylor, officially opened the course on the 24th May 1972. An eighteen-hole golf course along with a practice green, professionals shop and car-parking facilities, were completed by the Director of Public Works at a capital cost of £60,238.

The local government reorganisation, which took place on the 1st April 1974, saw Haigh become part of Wigan Metropolitan Borough. Haigh Hall and gardens were recognised as a valuable asset and top priority was given to their development as a leisure park.

Haigh Hall, 1904.

Haigh Hall viewed from the Leeds and Liverpool Canal which divides the park into the upper and lower plantations. Circa 1910.

James Ludovic, 26th Earl of Crawford, was born on the 28th July 1847. He married Emily Florence, daughter of the Honourable Edward Bootle-Wilbraham, on the 22nd July 1869. Amongst a number of public offices he held were M.P. for Wigan from 1874 to 1880 and Chairman of the Wigan Libraries Committee for thirty-five years. His death occurred on the 31st January 1913.

David Alexander Edward Lindsay
27th Earl of Crawford and 10th Earl of Balcarres.

Constance Lilian, daugher of Sir Henry Carstairs
Pelly, married Lord Balcarres in 1900.

Lord and Lady Balcarres with their chauffeur and family at Haigh Hall.

Postcard used in the Chorley Division Parliamentary Election of 1903, showing Alderman James Lawrence of Anderton Hall, the Liberal candidate, and Lord Balcarres of Haigh Hall, the Conservative candidate.

Wigan Royal Albert Edward Infirmary, circa 1910.
The Infirmary was opened by the Prince and Princess of Wales in 1873. The Royal couple stayed at Haigh Hall.

ENTERTAINING AT HAIGH HALL

Garden Party at Haigh Hall, 9th June 1906.

Lord Balcarres at Haigh Hall, 12th March 1908.

Lord Balcarres in conversation at Haigh Hall, 12th March 1908.

Visitors admire the view from the side of Haigh Hall while others are moving towards the marquee beside the carriage drive to the hall.

PRESS REPORTS

The Earl and Countess of Crawford and Family.

AT THE HAIGH PLOUGHING SOCIETY'S FOAL SHOW.

A HAPPY FAMILY GROUP.
THE EARL AND COUNTESS OF CRAWFORD AND FIVE OF THEIR EIGHT CHILDREN.
INCLUDING LORD BALNIEL, LADY MARGARET LINDSAY, LADY ANNE LINDSAY, LADY ELIZABETH LINDSAY, AND THE HON. JAMES LINDSAY.

The first public appearance of the Right Hon. the Earl of Crawford and Balcarres, since his recall from the Front and his appointment to the important office of President of the Board of Agriculture and Fisheries, was very appropriately made under the auspices of the Haigh, Aspull, and Blackrod Ploughing Society and Foal Show, of which his lordship is president, at the annual show, which as reported in our columns last week, was held on the Haigh estate on Saturday week, when Lord Crawford distributed the prizes to the successful exhibitors, and, referring to the war and agriculture, gave some advice to farmers. The Earl and Countess of Crawford, who are now in residence at Haigh Hall, with their children, spent some hours on the show ground, and the above group photograph, for which we are indebted to the "Preston Guardian," was taken on the field. The Earl and Countess, accompanied by their eight children, came on to the field as the judges were about to begin their tasks, and remained by the rope-lined ring until the final awards had been made. The family group, when the photograph was taken, was not complete, because of the fact that rain having set in, three of the younger children had returned to the hall.

ADVERTISER, SATURDAY. JUNE 3, 1933.

Lady Elizabeth Lindsay opens Haigh Church Bazaar.

J. Blackburn.

DEPUTISES FOR HER MOTHER.

Lady Elizabeth Lindsay opened a bazaar at Haigh School, in connection with the centenary of St. David's Church, Haigh, on Saturday afternoon, a report of which appears on another page. The picture was taken just before the opening ceremony, and shows Mr. J. A. Wood (Vicar's Warden), Rev. J. Schofield (Vicar), Lady Elizabeth Lindsay, Mr. A. M. Russell, and Mr. E. Armour (People's Warden). Lady Elizabeth deputised for her mother at the bazaar.

EARL OF CRAWFORD AT HAIGH CHURCH.

MR. NELSON, People's Warden.   Revd. G. P Plani   DR. DAVID Bishop   LORD CRAWFORD   Mr. Wood Vicars Warden

(Photograph by A. Lyons, Hindley.)

The Earl of Crawford attended the induction service at Haigh Parish Church, on Monday, when Rev. G. E. P. Cox was instituted Vicar of Haigh and Aspull. The Earl of Crawford is in the centre of the group with the Bishop of Liverpool, the new Vicar, officiating clergy and the churchwardens.

HAIGH HALL AND THE ESTATE BUILDINGS

There are many buildings dotted about the Haigh Estate, which were either occupied by staff or used in connection with the day to day running of its affairs. A selection of the properties is included to give some idea of the vast expense involved in servicing and maintaining such a property.

Haigh Hall

Haigh Hall from the carriage drive. Circa 1910. Prior to the First World War a staff of over twenty were responsible for running the hall.

Ivy Lane, Haigh. Circa 1910

LODGE HOUSES

Lodge Houses were situated at the various entrances to Haigh Park and were generally occupied by employees of the estate. The most imposing entranceway lodge is situated on Wigan Lane, Wigan, and is known locally as the Plantation Gates.

Plantation Gates, Wigan Lane, Wigan. 1909.

Whelley Lodge Gates. Circa 1919.

Lodge Gates, Aspull. 1905.
This property was known locally as Mow-Pin Lodge.

Basin Lane Lodge. 1904.

Estate Offices

Haigh Estate Offices. Circa 1905.
The stonework below the roof gable at the front contains the date 1892 which is probably the year of construction.
There is a small lodge situated opposite the Estate Office, which was used as a curling pond during the winter months.

Workshops

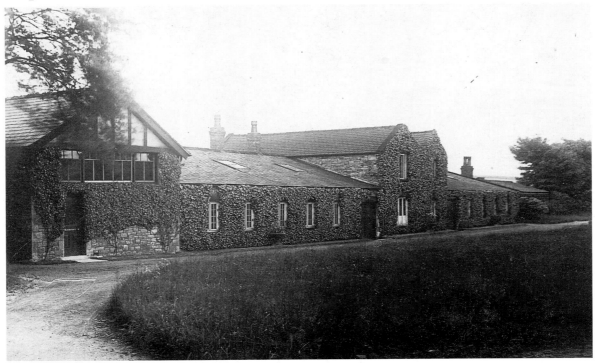

Haigh Estate Workshops. Circa 1910.
Built in the 1870s, the ivy covered workshops employed up to eighteen staff.

Haigh House

Haigh House, Haigh. Circa 1900.
Colonel Stanley Bell was a resident of this property during the 1930s/40s.
Haigh House was once occupied by the Sumner family who owned Haigh Brewery.

Haighlands

Haighlands, Haigh. Circa 1900.
Haighlands was constructed on the site of an old tannery, for Colin Lindsay, at a cost of £7,056.

Haigh Sawmills

Haigh Sawmills. Circa 1957. (Photo F. D. Smith)

The sawmills, built in 1839 were originally the workshop for Balcarres' Haigh and Aspull collieries. Following the formation of the Wigan Coal and Iron Company in 1865, the mills were mainly used for the collieries, the Kirkless Iron and Steel works, and for the requirements of Haigh Estate. A description of the complex which appears in the 'Industrial Archaeology of Lancashire' by Owen Ashmore (1969) describes the main buildings as running for 140 yards parallel to the canal, with east and west wings at right angles to the main block and a handsome Georgian style central office section with a roof cupola.

Curfew House

Curfew House, Haigh. Circa 1900.

Curfew House, Haigh, 1906.

Curfew House was situated next to a coal mine and the remains of the spoil heap are on the extreme left of this photograph. Apparently, there was a bell at the house which was rung as a time signal for the miners when the mine was being worked. This gave rise to the name of the property.

Haigh Hall. 2000

The Bothy, Haigh Estate, 2000.

All that remains of Haigh Sawmills is the central office section with the distinct roof cupola, which is now a private residence known as Sawmill Cottage. 2000.

Haigh Almshouses. 1995.
The Almshouses were originally built in 1772 at the expense of Dorothy, Lady Bradshaigh, in memory of her husband, Sir Roger Bradshaigh. The property, known as 'The Receptacle', was intended to house the poor, disabled and superannuated estate workers, servants or others deemed worthy. The property stood derelict in the 1970s but has since been restored for use as a private residence.

Close-up view of the tablet in the Almshouses which reads:-
"This receptacle for the benefit of the worthy poor was erected in 1772 at the expense of Dorothy, Lady Bradshaigh, relict of Sir Roger Bradshaigh, she thinking it the best way of shewing her gratitude and to perpetuate the memory of her affectionate husband, whose bounty enabled her to perform this act of charity as agreeable to his own good disposition".

Windmill Cottages, Copperas Lane, Haigh. 1995

Haigh Estate Dairy. 1995.
The property has been completely refurbished since this photograph was taken and is now in private ownership.

HAIGH PLANTATIONS

By the kindness of successive Earls of Crawford the general public have long enjoyed free access to Haigh plantations. Their popularity is shown to some extent by the large number of post card views which exist of the garden and recreation areas.

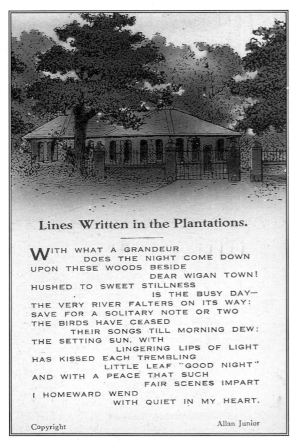

Lines Written in the Plantations.

WITH WHAT A GRANDEUR
                    DOES THE NIGHT COME DOWN
UPON THESE WOODS BESIDE
                    DEAR WIGAN TOWN!
HUSHED TO SWEET STILLNESS
                    IS THE BUSY DAY—
THE VERY RIVER FALTERS ON ITS WAY:
SAVE FOR A SOLITARY NOTE OR TWO
THE BIRDS HAVE CEASED
                    THEIR SONGS TILL MORNING DEW:
THE SETTING SUN. WITH
                    LINGERING LIPS OF LIGHT
HAS KISSED EACH TREMBLING
                    LITTLE LEAF "GOOD NIGHT"
AND WITH A PEACE THAT SUCH
                    FAIR SCENES IMPART
I HOMEWARD WEND
                    WITH QUIET IN MY HEART.

Copyright   Allan Junior

Since Wigan purchased the Haigh Estate in 1947, much effort and expenditure has been granted to maintain this extremely popular visitor attraction. At the time of writing the Haigh Golf Course is being extended and upgraded. The stables have been converted into a gallery/workshop with an information centre and cafe. Other attractions at Haigh Country Park include a miniature zoo and pets corner, walled gardens and a cactus house.

In addition to the recreational facilities provided by the Leeds and Liverpool Canal, there are 250 acres of mature woodland with 40 miles of secluded paths and trails making the amenity a haven for wildlife. It is one of the finest country parks in Britain.

A postcard published by Porter, Wigan, which was postally used on the 30th May 1934. This illustration appears to be the Basin Lane Lodge entrance to Haigh Hall.

Copperas Lane, Haigh. Circa 1900. Copperas Lane is the entrance to the plantations from Haigh village. Haigh School is the building on the left.

Copperas Lane, Haigh. Circa 1900. The lane to the left is Cow Lane and the cottages and buildings amongst the trees in the centre comprise the Home Farm.

Haigh Plantations, 1904.

Laurel Walk, Haigh Plantations. Circa 1905.

Haigh Plantations. 1958. A tractor/trailer, seen here on the right, commuted between Haigh Hall and the Plantation Gates on Wigan Lane, Wigan.

The greenhouses in the background were erected in 1846/47 and contained many exotic plants.

THE REST GARDENS, HAIGH HALL, WIGAN.

In front of the greenhouses was a lily pond filled with carp. It was a restful experience seeing the waters of the fountain playing on the surface of the pond, with the fish gliding gracefully among the water-lilies.

Douglas Bridge, Haigh Plantations.
1938

Inside the Plantation Gates.
Circa 1920.

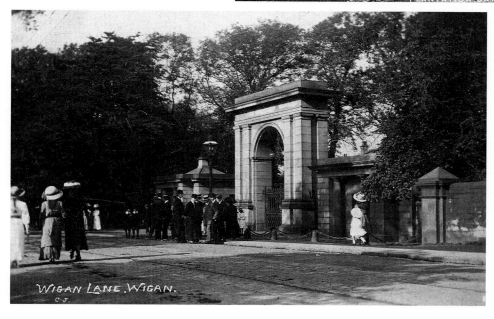

Visitors to Haigh Plantations dressed
in their Sunday Best. Circa 1910.

35

Gothic Cottages, Copperas Lane, Haigh. 1995.

Latham House (the old Estate Office) 1998.

Ian Lee's Professional Golf Shop, Haigh Hall Golf Course, 2000.

Re-construction of Haigh Golf Course is presently underway.

Heavy mechanical plant at work on the re-construction of Haigh Golf Course, 2000.

ST. DAVID'S CHURCH

St David's Church, Haigh and Aspull, is one of the 'Commissioners' churches built after 1819, when the Commissioners of the Treasury were authorised to issue Exchequer Bonds, not exceeding one million pounds, for church building. The basic purpose of the church building programme was to cater for the phenomenal growth of population in Lancashire at that time.

The first grant of £1m in 1819 financed the building of eighteen churches in the whole of Lancashire, whilst a second grant of £500,000 in 1825 facilitated the erection of a further 63 Lancashire churches. The difference resulted from the fact that the sums allowed for one church were much higher under the initial grant than the subsequent allocation.

Thomas Rickman was the architect for St David's Church and the building is described as having:- "Nave with bellcote and chancel. Long lancet windows, shafted inside with shaft rings. Wide interior, originally probably with galleries. The ceiling panelled with quatrefoils". Building costs were £3,433.

Work commenced in 1831, and the church of St David was opened on the 2nd June 1833. Bishop John Bird of Chester consecrated the church on the 28th November 1833.

Initially, the church was a Chapel-of-Ease, governed by the Rector of Wigan until 1838 when the Parish of Haigh and Aspull was formed. At this time the accommodation in the church is recorded as 796 seats of which 498 were 'free'.

In 1874 it was mooted that application be made to the Chancellor of the Diocese for the demolition of St. David's Church and the erection of a new and better building on the same, or some other site. This proposal was not further pursued.

Reverend C H James, who was the Vicar of Haigh from 1886 until 1918 successfully raised £3,055 by subscriptions, which enabled a Chancel to be added, the erection of two new vestries and the re-seating of the church. These additions were formally consecrated during 1887.

The first burial took place in 1834 and extensions were made to the graveyard in April 1867, March 1894 and during 1920. Several of the stained glass windows in the church were donated by local families in memory of their loved ones and the lych gate was erected in 1909 in memory of Henry Rawcliffe.

Three incumbents at St. David's Church appear on this photograph. Reverend C.H. James (1886-1918) is seated. Reverend Canon F.E. d'Anyers Willis (1918-1921) is standing back left with Reverend Canon A.C.W. Rose (1921-1922) back right.

Exterior view of St. David's Church, Haigh. Circa 1880.
At this time the chancel has not been added. Lord Balcarres provided stone for the church building from his quarry at Toddington and gave general support financially for the project.

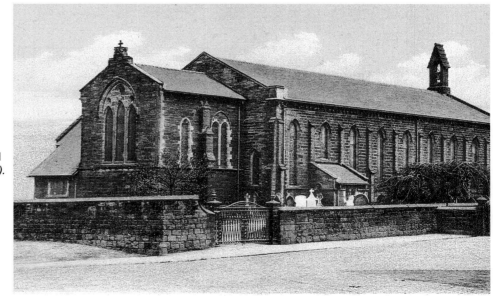

A chancel was added in 1886 designed by J. Medland Taylor. *(Photo circa 1909).*

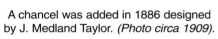

Interior of St. David's Church, Haigh. Circa 1925.

Haigh Vicarage. Circa 1925.

Haigh Vicarage. Circa 1907. Reverend C. H. James, Vicar of Haigh from 1886 until 1918 is standing in front with his daughters Madge and Phyllis. Lord Balcarres financed the building of the vicarage in the 1870s. It was subsequently demolished and replaced with a smaller property.

St. David's Church lych gate was erected in 1909 in memory of Henry Rawcliffe and this view shows the construction.
The contractors were Leonard Fairclough of Adlington. The walking day provides the main attraction on this occasion.

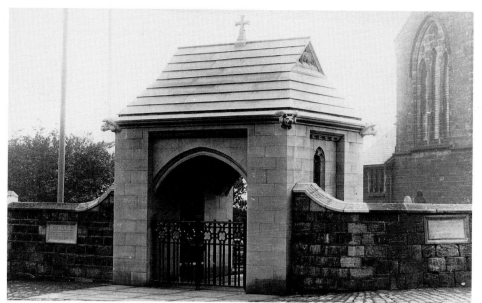

The completed lych gate. 1910.

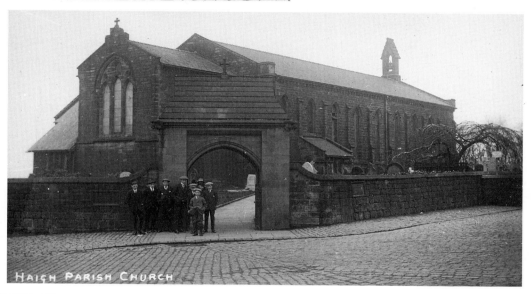

View of the church. Circa 1920.

HAICH PARISH CHURCH

GRANT, O Lord, that all who shall approach Thy House of Prayer through these gates, may come before Thee with pure thoughts and clean hearts, and serving Thee with reverence and godly fear may be acceptable in Thy sight; through Jesus Christ our Lord. *Amen.*

Office of Dedication

...of the...

Lych Gate

...at the...

Church of S. David,

Haigh and Aspull.

September 18th, 1909.

Within the Gateway on the East Wall is a Tablet of Copper, with raised letters, bearing the following inscription :—

TO THE GLORY OF GOD
AND IN AFFECTIONATE REMEMBRANCE
OF

HENRY RAWCLIFFE,

Who departed this life November 1st, 1907.

Aged 82 Years.

This Lychgate was erected by his Son:
A. W. R.

Details from the programme concerning the dedication of the lych gate at St. David's Church.

Commemorative stone tablet for the building of the lych gate. The inscription reads:-
ST. DAVID'S CHURCH, HAIGH
CHARLES HENRY JAMES, M.A., VICAR,
HENRY JAMES AINSWORTH AND
HENRY HEYES, CHURCH WARDENS IN THIS
YEAR OF GRACE 1909.

Commemorative datestone for two Church Wardens at St. David's Church, Haigh.

St. David's Church, Haigh. Circa 1920. On the photograph are shown the decorations in church for the wedding of Elsie Rawcliffe.

This unusual headstone marks the first burial in St. David's Churchyard, in 1834.
The inscription reads:

THIS GRANITE BOULDER WAS FOUND IN THIS CHURCHYARD WHILE A GRAVE WAS BEING DUG ABOUT THE YEAR 1878.
GEORGE EASTHAM. SEXTON
JOHN GIBSON. GRAVE-DIGGER
IT IS PLACED HERE TO MARK THE FIRST BURIAL IN 1834.
ERECTED 1910.
REVD. C.H. JAMES, VICAR
H.J. AINSWORTH
H. HEYES   CHURCH-WARDENS

St. David's Church, Haigh. Circa 1946.
These two photographs showing the church and lych gate were taken from the roof of Haigh Brewery by Ronald Dawson.

Interior of St. David's Church, Haigh. Circa 1950.

St. David's walking day – circa 1900. The girls' banner is being carried, this is no longer in use.

Reverend Howard Senar is on the right with a fellow clergyman. Churchwardens Fred Wood and Harry Winrow flank the two vicars. Procession circa 1950.

St. David's Church Choir descending the steps in front of Haigh School, 1946.
Reverend Bartlett leads the choir amongst whom are (from right to left): Vernon Jolly, Jimmy Riding, Ron Dawson, Roy Norton, Thomas Sanderson, Alan Miller, James Parr, John Carter, John Boardman, Kenneth Miller, Jack Churchouse, Jack Melling, William Melling and Harold Seddon.

St. David's Church organ, 2000.
Ron Dawson is seated at the organ. He has a long association with the church. Presently, it is an electronic organ and the organ pipes are no longer in use.

EDUCATION

In the History of Wigan, by David Sinclair published in 1882, is the following paragraph:-

HAIGH SCHOOL

"Haigh School was founded by Miles Sumer, according to his will dated 15th October 1634. He had been a tenant, or superior and successful servant, of Roger Bradshaigh, of Haigh, to whom he gave full power to carry out his testamentary instructions. He devised that, after all expenses, debts, and legacies had been paid, his remaining property should be divided into three parts, two of which should go for the immediate repair of Haigh roads and the perpetual benefit of the poor. A meeting of the inhabitants of Haigh decided that the money should be invested in lands, and the proceeds applied according to the testator's will. Accordingly, a farm in Billinge, called 'Outley-snape,' was purchased, and the public school built and endowed for the teaching of children whose parents should be inhabitants of, or possessed of lands or tenements or contributed to the lays in the said township of Haigh".

OLD HAIGH SCHOOL,

Old Haigh School, Circa 1910. The building stands on School Lane, near to the Red Rock entrance to Haigh Estate. A datestone, reading 1901, is situated above the doorways in the centre. At this time the building seems to have been refurbished and is in private occupation.

HAIGH SCHOOL

Haigh School was delayed in completion due to bricklayers taking industrial action. It was eventually completed in 1846 and the datestone at the front, below the sundial, confirms this.

Haigh School, circa 1910.
The school is formally entitled 'ST. DAVID, HAIGH AND ASPULL C.E. PRIMARY SCHOOL'.
For a period until 1879 the headmaster acted as a postmaster, transacting business from a window.
Until 1911, an allowance of free beer and coal was also afforded the headmaster.

Aspull Temperance Band on the steps of Haigh School on walking day. Circa 1925.

Old Haigh School, 1946.

St. David, Haigh and Aspull C.E. Primary School, 1995.

Haigh School, 1911.
Second from the left on the back row is Elizabeth Pendlebury.
On the second row, 5th from the left is Catherine (Cora) Pendlebury, with Mary Prescott and Lily Prescott 7th and 8th from the left respectively. John Pendlebury is third left on the front row.

St. David's School, Haigh, 1948.
The class comprises (left to right):
Back row: Peter Pinnington, James Sherrington, Joan Pendlebury, Lillian Wood, Jack Nelson, Raymond Hart.
Middle row: Ronnie Rudd, Roy Bolton, Colin Miller, James Bolton, David Kay, Irvine Pallister, John Carter, Clifford Edwards.
Front row: Muriel Kay, Ann Gaskell, Florence Postlethwaite, Margaret Halliwell, Eileen Heyes, Elsie Pollitt, Kathleen Parr.

Haigh C. of E. School, 1953.
Seated at the front, from left to right are: 1. James Lancaster. 4 David Parkinson.
On the back row (l to r) are: 1. Gordon Parr. 2. Bill Dobson. 5. Brian Rainford. 6. Alan Hart Wood.
Second row (l to r): 1. John Farrington. 3. Joyce Miller. 4. John Pendlebury. 5. Ann Weaver.
Front row standing (l to r): 3. Linda Brayshaw. 4. Brenda Brayshaw. 5 Sylvia Ince. 7. Joan Smith. 9. Margaret Hill.

RED ROCK C. of E. SCHOOL.

Red Rock School was built in the 1870's for Alexander William the 25th Earl of Crawford. He was a great scholar who had many of his works published. He spent much time in Italy where he purchased and refurbished a villa near Florence.

Red Rock C. of E. School, 1975.

Red Rock School, 1921. Identification for the class photograph is on the slate held by the boy seated front right.

Red Rock School, Red Rock Lane, 2000. The old school is no longer in use and has been converted into a private dwelling house.

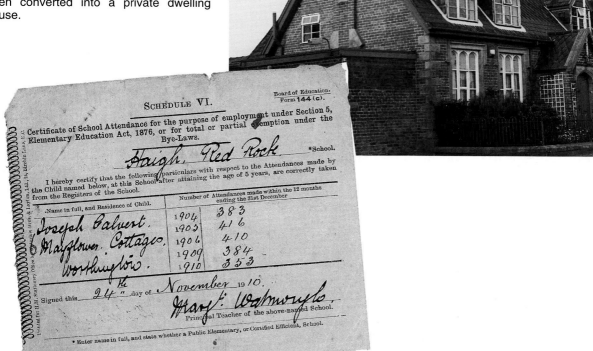

School attendance record for the year 1904-1910 in respect of Joseph Calvert, 6 Mayflower Cottages, Worthington. Mary (or Margaret) Watmough has signed this red Rock School record as principal teacher.

51

HAIGH BREWERY

Haigh Brewery was a five storey building which stood behind the Balcarres Arms. A series of cellar areas were located beneath the brewery. One of the cellars extended under the nearby Haigh School, while another was connected by a tunnel under the road to a location beneath Sumner's Row. Brewing was commenced by John Sumner in the 1820's, in conjunction with the Balcarres Arms. The five storey brewery was constructed in 1873.

There is need for a great deal of water in the brewing process and a water well, forty feet deep, was situated in the brew house from where the water was channelled for use.

A windmill still stands in the fields off Copperas Lane which was at one time used for pumping water to the brewery.

In recollections of working at Haigh Brewery, Mr J F Moore, who died in 1982, remembers a huge water tank, 15 feet square by 8 feet deep, situated some 30 feet above ground level, which was filled with water from a lodge in fields behind the brewery. In an effort to conserve clean water from the town's supply, the lodge water was used for such jobs as swilling down initially before finishing with clean water.

A malt kiln existed off Bolton Road, Aspull, which had under-floor heating to assist in germination and growth of the grain. The building was, apparently, four storeys high and after falling into disuse was demolished.

Raw materials for brewing included sugar, hops and malt; which were transported to Haigh from Liverpool, Kent, and Lincoln, respectively.

A sophisticated network of mineral railway lines connected the various collieries in Blackrod, Aspull and Haigh. These mineral lines joined the main rail routes and it was by this means that raw materials were delivered and goods despatched. Rawcliffe Sidings at Aspull was the delivery point for Haigh Brewery. The various goods would be off-loaded onto horse drawn transport for the final leg of the journey to the brewery.

In the days before motor transport, up to 45 shire horses and 4 ponies were in the employ of Haigh Brewery. They were kept busy servicing numerous retail outlets, carting fuel and supplies, and carrying materials for repair work, etc. A staff of 25 carters, 2 blacksmiths and a harness mender were responsible for the animals, with a Mr Rawcliffe in overall charge of operations. Motor transport was eventually introduced and the need for horses gradually diminished.

In the Wigan Directory for 1869, there are references to Henry Rawcliffe, brewer (John Sumner and Co.) and John Sumner and Co., brewers and spirit merchants. The Rawcliffe and Sumner families were connected by marriage and although there was not a separate Rawcliffe Company, the family owned property and traded under the Sumner name. On the 31st May 1919, following the death of Augustus Walter Rawcliffe, the two concerns were merged.

Greenalls Group took over many of the Sumner outlets in the 1930's although the actual date of the transfer of John Sumner Ltd, to Greenall Whitley, was the 7th June 1955.

Haigh Brewery, circa 1900.

This excellent photograph of the brewery shows what a large concern the business of John Sumner was locally. In the arch of the brickwork above the loading bays is the date 1873, which is probably the date of construction.

Haigh Brewery ceased to be operational following the takeover of its outlets by Greenalls, and the property was demolished by E Calderbank and Sons Ltd., of Orchard Street, Wigan, in the 1950's.

John and Helen Sumner are buried along with their son and daughter in Horwich Parish Church graveyard. It seems that William, their 11 year old son, was killed in an accident whilst working for his father at the brewery on the 21st December 1839. His sister, Jane, died in infancy on the 31st July 1841 aged just 21 days.

John Sumner died on the 13th December 1867 aged 69 years, and his wife, Helen, on the 30th April 1883, aged 79 years.

Haigh Windmill, circa 1910.
The windmill was used for pumping water to Haigh Brewery.

Farming near to the windmill. Circa 1910.

Work people and their families ready for a days outing in a char-a-banc. The following are among the passengers: Mr & Mrs Knowles, Mr & Mrs Duffy, Mr & Mrs Lee, Mr & Mrs Owen, Mr & Mrs Wood, Misses Trainers, Ellen Seddon, Annie Smith, Rebecca Culshaw and Mrs Pimblett. Haigh Brewery's malt kiln is in the background. Circa 1920.

Haigh Brewery, 1920.
The brewery is in the centre of this old walking day photograph.

Letter head for Haigh Brewery, 1886.

Letter head, 1892.

John Sumner's Brewery wagon photographed on Chorley New Road, Lostock, Bolton. The vehicle was built by Fred Wood of Culraven House, Haigh.

Brass tokens were in use by several pubs and were accepted as money. The rubbings (above) are of tokens used in the Balcarres Arms, Haigh and Top Lock Inn, Aspull.

(left) Bottle label for Sumner's Light Dinner Ale.

An Aerial view of Haigh Road. Circa 1960, Culraven Garage is in the centre of this view with Haigh House on the top right. Culraven House is the detached property bottom right. On the far left is the Balcarres Arms, with Haigh School behind. The School sports ground is top centre, with goal posts. Haigh Brewery has been demolished but the site is still visible between the Balcarres Arms and Culraven Garage.

Two views of Haigh Brewery yard taken from the five storey brewery roof. In the top picture the wall on the right is behind Haigh House. Dereliction of the buildings in the brewery yard is evident.

THE SUMNER FAMILY VAULT IN HORWICH PARISH CHURCH GRAVEYARD.

The text reads: "Sacred to the Memory of William son of John & Helen Sumner, who unfortunately lost his life whilst doing the will of his father December 21st 1839, in the 11th year of his age. Also of Jane, their infant daughter who died July 31st 1841, aged 21 days".

On the oppopsite side is the following legend: "Sacred to the Memory of John Sumner, of Haigh House, who died December 13th 1867, aged 69 years. Blessed are the dead which die in the Lord, they rest from their labour, and their works do follow them.
Also of Helen, his wife, who entered into rest April 30th 1883, aged 79 years.

    Not gone from memory
    Not gone from love
    But at rest for ever,
    In the home above.
And their children arise and call them blessed.

HAIGH FOUNDRY

Several iron furnaces and forges were operating in South Lancashire during the eighteenth century, including two forge sites on the River Douglas, near Wigan, at Bottlingwood and Brock respectively. The forge at Brock later became part of the Haigh Ironworks.

Brock Mill Forge, on the River Douglas, was advertised for sale in 1766, and in 1775 another nearby forge was also offered for sale due to the owner, a Mr James of Wigan, being declared bankrupt.

On the 20th August 1788, Alexander, the 23rd Earl of Crawford and the 6th Earl of Balcarres, entered into a partnership with James Corbett an iron founder of Wigan, and his brother Robert Lindsay, who at the time was in India, to set up furnaces at Leyland Mill, Haigh. The concern was to include Brock Mill Forge, which was sold to the partnership for £400. The company traded as Lindsay, Corbett and Company.

Robert Lindsay was eminently qualified to make a success of the partnership. He had vast experience in trade, having been in the service of the East India Company and had amassed wealth in India in occupations as diverse as lime manufacturer, tiger-hunter, elephant-catcher, ship-builder and ornamental gardener. His brother, Earl Lindsay, provided the commercial capital for the scheme.

James Corbett, who was the original owner of the foundry at Brock Mill, had grandiose plans for expansion. In 1789 he proposed the setting up of a boring-mill capable of boring seven cylinders of different diameters or six pieces of cannon, at one time. However he died in 1790 and it soon became obvious that he had been responsible for wasting considerable capital.

Although Robert Lindsay was reluctant to live at Haigh on his return from India, he was keen to protect his investment in the partnership. He took responsibility for hiring and firing staff at the foundry and eventually established a reliable workforce. The works themselves were not neglected. A weir was repaired, the construction of a casting house was commenced and tenements were provided for the men, with stabling for the horses.

By 1790, Haigh Iron Works was a viable concern. An advertisement in a Liverpool newspaper offered the services of a Blast Furnace and Boring Mill at Haigh, together with the skills necessary to construct Fire Engines of every kind.

In 1793 the partnership involving Haigh Iron Works was officially dissolved. It then began trading as James Lindsay and Company.

A succession of bad managers did irreparable damage to the company. Joseph Von Baader seems to have impressed Robert Lindsay with his abilities, but proved totally unreliable and deceitful. He introduced workers from Germany who smashed the moulding patterns to make furniture, and miners he employed did very little work, starting late and finishing early. He was eventually dismissed.

Alexander Haliburton of Inverkeithing was appointed as manager in January 1793. He retained his position until 1823 or 1824, when bad debts amounting to almost £24,000 came to light. It seems that Haliburton had personal interests in mines and a copperas (Ferrous Sulphate) works.

One result of such mismanagement was that the furnaces were de-commissioned in 1815 and demolished in 1828. Work was then centred on the foundry and engineering works. Products included paddle shaft for steamboats, wrought iron work for churches and locomotives.

Haigh Foundry was well known for producing large castings but the difficulty in transporting the products made them expensive. Up to thirty horses, yoked in pairs, were required to haul the castings up Leyland Mill Lane, with at least twelve horses to pull the load to Wigan. Amongst the contracts fulfilled were cast iron tubings and arches for the first railway Mersey Tunnel and the famous Laxey Wheel made to pump water from the lead mines at Laxey in the Isle of Man. Lady Isabella Hope, wife of the Governor of the Isle of Man set the Laxey Wheel in motion in 1854. Although the wheel was damaged by floodwater in 1930, it was subsequently reconditioned and still provides a popular visitor attraction. It is said that a hundred horses were needed to pull the Laxey Wheel up Leyland Mill Lane.

Tom Sharrock from Haigh Foundry accompanied the wheel to the Isle of Man to supervise the erection.

Not all the employees were unreliable. A father and son, both named Robert Daglish, worked hard to improve the engineering side of the business. A successful venture was the manufacture of the first Lancashire locomotive, known as the 'Walking Horse', which was modelled on Blenkinsop's 'Yorkshire Horse'. Locomotive manufacture continued until 1856 when the firm began to concentrate on mining machinery.

Earl Lindsay sold out the business in 1835 to Messrs Evans, Ryley and Burrows on a 21-year lease. It was then taken over by another partnership, Messrs Birley and Robert Thompson. The former company was responsible for the construction of 114 locomotives at Haigh, while the latter concentrated on mining machinery and traded as Haigh Foundry Co., Wigan.

A rail link was established around 1860 which connected Haigh Foundry and Brock Mill Forge to the existing railway system in the neighbourhood of the Lindsay Pits and the main line railway system.

Frederick Henry Birley joined the partnership of Henry Birley and Robert Thompson in 1859.

On the 28th April 1877, it was mooted that the Birleys took over Haigh Foundry and Thompson take over Brook Mill Forge. It is not clear whether or not the business split was ever introduced but possibly not.

Both Haigh Foundry and Brock Mill Forge were advertised for let in November 1883, and again in January 1884. There were no takers. The result was that in January 1885 it was publicly announced that the Haigh Foundry Company was giving up business, being unable to match the competition.

Haigh Foundry premises were taken over by J J Petford Ltd., who manufactured bedsteads. The firm went into receivership in October 1908. Since this time a variety of light engineering firms have used the old foundry which continues to the present day.

Brock Mill Forge was converted for use as a textile printing and dyeing works in the 1880's and operated in this capacity until bankruptcy forced closure in the 1930's. The new owner of the Forge, James Harvey, arranged for the removal of the railway sidings operated at the works.

A variety of manufacturing concerns now operate in the area where the old Haigh Foundry stood. There are few clues as to its previous use, other than the bridgework carrying Leyland Mill Lane over the valley of the River Douglas, which contain both a 1796 and an 1846 datestone.

Brock Mill Forge has long since been demolished and a relatively modern factory complex, producing plastic pipework, now occupies the site.

Brock Mill Cottages have disappeared and all that remains are the distinctive seventy steps, which bear evidence of frequent past use but now seem out of place in a deserted woodland setting.

Views of the Brock Mill and Leyland Mill areas are included dating from about 1900. Although the district is, strictly speaking, in Wigan; the ownership of much of the property once rested with the Earls of Crawford and Balcarres of Haigh Hall.

It is interesting to visit the area to compare the old photographs with present day conditions although, understandably, access is somewhat restricted because of private property ownership.

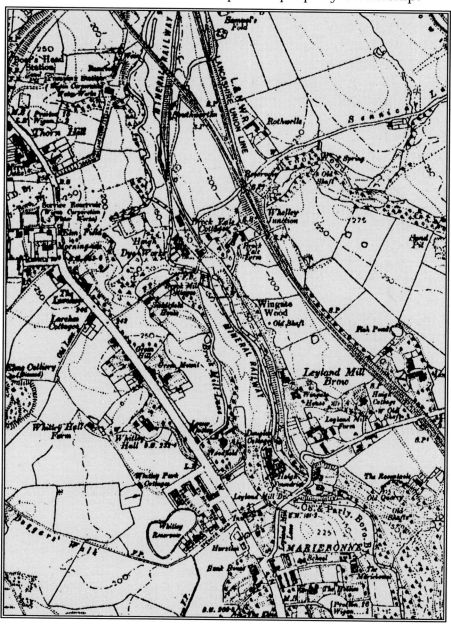

Map of the Brock Mill and Leyland Mill areas. Circa 1900.

61

BROCK MILL AND LEYLAND MILL AREAS

View in Brock Mill, 1905.

View of Leyland Mill Lane, showing the bridge parapet, which contains an 1846 datestone, on the left. Haigh Foundry entrance is on the right and the works were reached by travelling under the bridge and to the left.

BROCK MILL COTTAGES

Brockmill Cottages, circa 1900.
The bridge on the left carried the old mineral railway line over the River Douglas.

Brockmill Cottages, circa 1935.

BROCKMILL COTTAGES.

G.BT09.

Brockmill Cottages, circa 1920.
On the left can be seen the old mineral railway bridge with the trackbed bare of rail lines.

Despite the caption on this postcard view – 'Brockmill Cottage, Wigan Nov. 5.11 – it has not been possible, up to the present time, properly to identify the property.

General multi-view card of Brockmill.

Snowscape in Brockmill, 1936.

Brockmill sledge-run, 1936.

CAST IRON MILESTONES

Cast-iron milestone plates and cast-iron milestones on the A49 and A5106 in the Standish area were made at Haigh Foundry in Wigan in 1837. The naming of the parish or township was not usual on the stone until the beginning of the nineteenth century and was never a legal requirement.

Cast iron milestone on the A49 opposite the Boar's Head Hotel at Standish.

Situated on the A5106 near to Standish Bleachworks, this cast iron milestone is showing signs of neglect.

INDUSTRIAL MACHINERY

This cast iron plate was taken from a wagon-lift at London Road Railway Station, Manchester, during demolition.

There are two datestones in the Leyland Mill Lane Bridge. The one on the left reads 1846 and the one on the right 1796.

This bridge carries Leyland Mill Lane over the Haigh Foundry yard. 2000.

Leyland Mill Lane. 2000.
On the right is the entrance to what was Haigh Foundry.

Site of the old Haigh Foundry. 2000.
At the present time the following firms occupy the site:

1. Jeffreys Miller & Co. Ltd.
2. Potters (Herbal Supplies) Ltd.
3. Haigh Investment Co. Ltd.
4. Itona Products Ltd.
5. Haigh Development Co. Ltd.
6. Worsley Chemical Co. Ltd.
7. Sea Products (Wigan) Ltd.
8. Hamblo Plastics Ltd.
9. Westmorland Chocolate Ltd.

Brock Mill Cottages. 2000.
Several properties are referred to as Brock Mill Cottages which causes confusion. On an old map these cottages are shown as Brock Vale Cottages.

River Douglas, Brock Mill.

Bridge over the River Douglas from the old Brock Mill
Forge (now a plastics factory) to Brock Mill Cottages
(now demolished). 2000.
The mineral line railway bridge was situated further
upstream towards Leyland Mill.

Seventy-steps, Brock Mill. 2000

THE LAXEY WHEEL

The Laxey Wheel was designed by Robert Casement, who had been appointed Superintendent Engineer to the Laxey Mining Company in 1848. A variety of valuable mineral deposits were mined in the area of Laxey, including lead (with silver) and zinc. There were many other mines in the locality, some of which employed water wheels. It is also known that a water wheel operating at the Great Laxey Mine in 1828 was augmented by a larger wheel in 1840. This second wheel was not sufficient to pump out water from the mines, hence the decision to design an even larger wheel - the Laxey Wheel.

Statistically, the Laxey Wheel is 228 feet in circumference, with a diameter of 72 feet 6 inches and a width of 6 feet. The axle is 17 feet long with a diameter of 21 inches and weighing 10 tons.

Many publications in Wigan, particularly successive guides to Haigh Hall and a Bulletin of the John Rylands Library on The Haigh Ironworks (1789 - 1856) by Alan Birch, M.A., clearly state that the Laxey Wheel was "cast, forged, built and completed at Haigh Foundry".

In the latest guide to "Lady Isabella" and the Great Laxey Mine, jointly published by The Manx Experience and The Manx Museum and National Trust; the construction of the Laxey Wheel axle and cranks is credited to The Mersey Iron Works, Ellesmere Port, whilst the giant hubs were reportedly supplied by the Vauxhall Foundry, Liverpool.

There has been much correspondence over the years to the Wigan Observer newspaper , supplying proof that the Laxey Wheel was built at Haigh Foundry. A Mr E Bradley, of 25 Thomas Street, Garston wrote to the editor, "I cannot understand there being any doubt about the Laxey Wheel having been made in Wigan. I remember it being brought down from the Haigh Foundry one early morning on its way to the island. My father was then the licensee of the old Dog-ith'-Thatch, Wigan. A lot of the men who worked on the wheel used to frequent the house." Mr T L Lance, J.P., of Wigan, himself a Manxman, wrote several times on the subject in an effort to confirm the Haigh connection with the Laxey Wheel. Mrs Eleanor Prestt of 42 Avondale Road, Wigan - also entered the debate. She said that her late father, Mr James Ellis, moved from Hawarden to Haigh in November 1867 and worked at the foundry until its closure. Her father often spoke of the Laxey Wheel having been built at Haigh Foundry.

Whilst there is no definite proof to confirm the construction of the Laxey Wheel at Haigh Foundry, it seems an odd claim to make.

One explanation, rebutting the claim is that it is more likely that the wheel built at Haigh Foundry was the "Elizabeth", which was used in the North Laxey Mines in the next valley. This was an all metal wheel, much smaller than the Laxey Wheel.

Whatever the case it is a contentious issue which still remains unresolved after nearly one hundred and fifty years.

Laxey Water Wheel and Village. I. o. M.

Laxey Wheel and village, Isle of Man. Circa 1938.
The Great Laxey Mine was closed in 1920. An auction was arranged for the mine to be dismantled but a local businessman, Mr Robert Williamson, bought the mine just before the auction sale scheduled for April 1922. Attempts to keep the mine open failed and the Williamson family had to admit defeat closing the mine for good in 1929. It was subsequently purchased by Mr Edwin Kneale who eventually sold it to the Manx Government in 1965.

Laxey Wheel As An Isle of Man Asset

The people of Laxey in the Isle of Man have organised a petition asking for a public meeting to be convened to consider the future of the famous Laxey Wheel, which, after becoming derelict, is now regarded as a real asset to the island. The big wheels, which was made in Wigan over eighty years ago, was built to pump water out of the Laxey Lead mines, which are not now worked, and the Wheel has ceased to turn. Its great value nowadays is as an object of interest to visitors, and it is felt that if the Wheel is to be idle permanently not only Laxey but the Isle of Man as a whole will lose thereby. Hence the move to ensure it going round again even if the mines are not working. It is interesting to recall that it was at the old Haigh Foundry, Wigan, that the Laxey Wheel was made, and at Haigh Foundry there were three water wheels used to turn the machinery of the foundry, which a hundred years ago was famous all over the world for its huge castings, some of which weighed over thirty tons. These huge castings had to be drawn up the steep road from the foundry by horse power, and many old Wiganers can recall hearing their parents tell of the long teams of horses required to transport the tremendous loads. It is quite probably that the idea of utilising a giant wheel to pump the water from the lead mines at Laxey was suggested by the water wheels already in operation at Haigh Foundry before the Laxey Wheel was made there.

Famous Manx Landmark Threatened

Laxey Wheel, the famous Isle of Man landmark, which, it is reported, may have to go, was, it is interesting to recall, made at the old Haigh Foundry, Wigan. The restoration of the wheel, so it is said, would cost the Laxey ratepayers, a sixpenny rate, and the village council are not disposed to impose this burden. The only chance of the wheel being saved appears to be for the Manx Government to step in. The wheel was built in 1854 to draw water from the Laxey lead mines. It was then the largest wheel in the world, measuring 226 feet in circumference, with 188 buckets, and drawing up to 300 gallons of water a minute from the mine. The mine has become derelict, and the wheel has not turned for two years. Unless extensive restoration is carried out, it is not likely to turn again. The wheel, in its day, has brought millions of visitors to Laxey, and Laxey people view with dismay the prospect of losing this well-established attraction. Probably more pictures of Laxey Wheel are sold to adorn Lancashire homes than any other holiday view. The late Mr. Samuel Melling, J.P., the Wigan engineer, who died last year at the age of ninety, and had interesting recollections of Haigh Foundry, which was working when he was a boy, believed that Laxey Wheel was made at the Wigan Foundry in 1853, and there used to be an old Wiganer named Tom Sharrock, who was never tired of telling the part he played in the casting and the erection of the 'big wheel' of Manxland.

The Dog i'th Thatch pub, Wigan Lane, Wigan. Circa 1870.
The licensee at this time is named Maycock. A previous tenant named Bradley remembered the
Laxey Wheel being brought into Wigan from Haigh Foundry (see newspaper reports above).

BOUNDARY MARKERS

Haigh Triangle, 2000.
Haigh Triangle is marked by the raised cobblestones with a tree growing in the centre. It is situated next to the Balcarres Arms and marks the convergence of three ecclesiastical districts, namely the Blackburn, Liverpool and Manchester Diocese.
Reverend Senar adopted the practice of blessing the village of Haigh from the triangle on Rogation Sunday.

This stone boundary marker, situated outside St. David's Church, is inscribed on the left face "Hundred of Salford – Township of Aspull".
On the right hand face is contained the legend "Hundred of West Derby – Township of Haigh".

Haigh Road, showing the two signs for Haigh and Aspull near to the lych gate for St. David's Church.

ORIGIN OF THE NAME ASPULL

Aspull is derived from the Old English 'aesp-leah', which translates to 'aspen wood'. The Book of Fees for 1212 contains a reference to Aspul, whilst the Assize Rolls for 1246 mention Aspull.

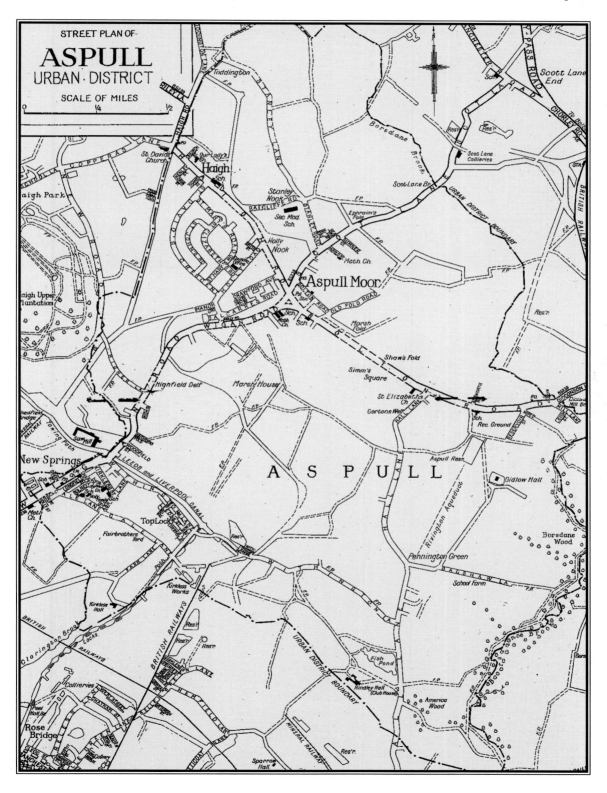

Borsdane Brook, Borsdane Wood. Circa 1930.
Borsdane Brook forms a natural boundary between Aspull and Westhoughton. It flows through Borsdane Wood,
which was originally part of the land belonging to Hindley Hall comprising some 65 acres.

Hindley Hall. 2000. Hindley Hall is situated in Aspull and in 1664 was the seat of James Dukenfield,
a barrister. The present building dates from about 1767 and was the residence of Roger Leigh in
the 1870's. It is presently the club house for Hindley Golf Course.

THE MANOR OF ASPULL

Although Aspull is situated in the Parish of Wigan it is in the hundred of Salford, while Wigan lies in the hundred of West Derby.

In the survey of 1212, Aspull comprised one of a total of 6½ plough-lands held chiefly by Richard de Lathom, and partly by Roger de Samlesbury and Alexander de Harwood. The lands formed part of the Childwall fee, and were held under the Lord of Manchester.

Immediately after this time, lands in Aspull are referred to as being in the possession of William de Notton. He held them with the assent of Cecily, his wife, daughter of Edith, lady of Barton-on-Irwell. They formed part of her dower. Although the holdings of the Lathoms in Aspull are not mentioned, they do receive recognition in 1290.

Richard de Ince, son and heir of Henry de Sefton, and Adam de Hindley, held Aspull in 1302 as the eighth part of a Knight's fee, directly from Thomas Grelley, Lord of Manchester. The tenants were bound to contribute to the maintenance of the bailiff of the Manchester barony.

The grandson of Richard de Ince left a daughter and heir, Ellen, who married John, the third son of Sir Peter Gerard of Bryn, in about 1386. John and Ellen made a settlement of the manor of Aspull in 1421.

Thomas Gerard held the lordship of Aspull in 1473, from the Lord of Manchester, for a rent of eight pence, whilst in 1558 Miles Gerard held Aspull, for a rental of eighteen pence, for Lord La Warre.

Until the early years of the 18th century, Aspull and Ince were held conjointly but Ince was sold by Richard, son of Thomas Gerard of Highfield, to the Gerards of Bryn.

Sir William Gerard was lord of the manor of Aspull in 1796. It was eventually sold to the Earl of Crawford and Balcarres before 1825.

Ownership of part of Aspull was vested in the Hindley family, who appear to have held a quarter of the manor by the grant of William, son of Richard, son of Enot de Aspull. Succession can be traced from Adam, son of Hugh de Hindley, who was living in 1292, until the 17th century, when Roger Hindley came into possession of the property.

Hindley Hall was the seat of the Hindley family and it eventually became the property of James, a younger son of Robert Dukinfield of Cheshire. The Leighs of Whitley Hall, Wigan, acquired Hindley Hall in the 18th century. Sir Robert Holt Leigh lived there until his death on the 21st January 1843. Sir Robert's cousin, Thomas Pemberton, inherited the estate. He adopted the name Leigh, becoming Thomas Pemberton Leigh, and chose Hindley Hall as his residence. He was elevated to the peerage, becoming Baron Kingsdown, in 1858.

Lands in Aspull were held from an early period by the Knights Hospitallers. In rent records for 1540, the following four tenements are mentioned in this connection:- one messuage held by Thomas Gorsuch, Occleshaw, by Alexander Catterall, Whittington House, by John Byrom, and a messuage by William Houghton. Occleshaw and Whittington House are, of course, properties. In 1276 the prior of St. John of Jerusalem was claimant against John de Occleshaw and another. Occleshaw was eventually acquired by the Ince family.

Gidlow Hall is another old property associated with the history of Aspull. Robert de Gidlow held the freehold of certain lands in Aspull in 1291 and the name appears frequently until the 17th century.

Highfield House was once used by local Roman Catholics for religious services and eventually became a farming property; while Kirklees is another old residence in Aspull which was for many centuries the home of the Houghtons.

Local government came to Aspull in 1876 with the formation of a Local Board and in 1894 Aspull Urban District Council was formed.

Aspull presently lies in the Wigan Metropolitan District of the County of Greater Manchester, which was formed during the local government re-organisation which became effective on the 1st April 1974.

ASPULL URBAN DISTRICT COUNCIL
1894-1974

Councillor William Maunders, Chairman
and Members of the Council

have pleasure in inviting

Miss H. Weaver. & friend

to the

Official Opening of the Aspull Civic Hall

Woods Road, Aspull

by PETER RYDER, Esq., former Clerk of the Council
at 7-30 p.m., on Friday, 29th March, 1974

to be followed by a Social Evening commemorating 80 years of
Local Government Service to the people of the Urban District

Dress Informal

R.S.V.P. to the Clerk of the Council,
Council Offices, Aspull, Wigan.
by 22nd March, 1974.

Dancing 8-15 p.m. to midnight
Buffet 9-30 p.m.
A Bar will be available.

Invitation to the opening of Aspull Civic Hall on Friday, 29th March, 1974. The crest of Aspull Urban District Council, shown at the top left, contains an ostrich, which forms part of the Earl of Crawford's Coat of Arms.

On Thursday, 15th October, 1942, the Earl of Crawford presented a chain of office for the Chairman of Aspull Urban District Council. The chain, which has twenty-five silver gilt links, has a pendant comprising a rose worked in red, the word 'Chairman' in enamel, and then the crest of the Council, an ostrich. 'Aspull District Council, Lancashire, 1894', is inscribed on the pendant. A public subscription was opened by the town clerk in May 1942, and such was the response that not only were they able to obtain a pendant but a chain as well.

Left to right on the photograph are:– Mr. L. Abbott (Clerk), the Earl of Crawford, Councillor J. Higham (Chairman), the Mayor of Wigan – Councillor R. Prestt. J.P., and Robert Weaver (Vice-Chairman, Aspull Council).

Aspull Council Offices. 2000

ASPULL URBAN DISTRICT COUNCIL ELECTION
MONDAY, 5th APRIL, 1937

....

TO THE ELECTORS OF NORTH WARD

....

Ladies and Gentlemen,

It is my pleasure to remind you that the LOCAL COUNCIL ELECTION is here again, and a selection will be made on MONDAY, 5th APRIL, 1937, as to the Candidate whom you think will be a REPRESENTATIVE most suitable for your requirements.

I have been asked at various times, over a period of several years, to allow my name to come before the people of ASPULL for their consideration, but owing to other ties I have not felt free to do so.   Now, I have more time to spare and feel that I can more conscientiously devote my energies to Council work ; and I ask to place my name before you for your kind choice.

There is no need for me to tell you who I am, for I have lived amongst you all my life, and worked with you in more than one sphere of activity.

I express my true feelings when I say that I am sincerely interested, and always have been in the welfare of Aspull and its inhabitants.   It seems to be usual for a Candidate to say that he will try to further the progress of HOUSING, UNEMPLOYMENT, CHILD WELFARE, EDUCATION, and other schemes.   I AM PREPARED TO SUPPORT ANY CAUSE MEETING THE NEEDS OF ASPULL—THE DISTRICT AND THE PEOPLE SHALL HAVE MY GREATEST CONSIDERATION AT ALL TIMES.

If you should honour me with your verdict on MONDAY, 5th APRIL next, I shall endeavour to be worthy of your trust by acting in an honest, straightforward manner on behalf of the District, and to your best interests.

I will leave it to your decision.

I am,

Ladies and Gentlemen,

Yours faithfully,

ROBERT WEAVER

2 Stanley Road,
Aspull.

No. 2 ON THE BALLOT PAPER

Polling Station :

METHODIST SCHOOL, FINGER POST

5th APRIL, 1937, from 12 noon to 8 p.m.

Printed and Published by James Risley Ltd., Platt Lane, Scholes, Wigan. Tel. 3559

ROBERT WEAVER
BORN 21ST NOVEMBER 1878 AT ASPULL

Robert Weaver, who followed John Higham as Chairman of Aspull U.D.C., with his wife Annie (nee Southern) and daughter Hannah. Circa 1904.

Hannah Weaver with her two brothers, William (left) and John. Circa 1913.

View from the front of No. 2 Stanley Road, Aspull, family home of the Weavers. Circa 1950.

Robert Weaver as President of the Independent
Order of Oddfellows.

Robert and Annie Weaver in St. David's Churchyard,
with Haigh School in the background.

CHURCHES

OUR LADY'S CHURCH, HAIGH ROAD, ASPULL

The foundation stone for Our Lady's Church, Haigh Road, Aspull was laid on St. Joseph's Feast 1857. The church was officially opened on the 25th April, 1858, with the celebration of Pontifical High Mass.

A presbytery was added in 1862 and further alterations were carried out in 1871.

On completion of the church, it was described as being decorated in early English style and of dimensions 104 feet long by 40 feet wide. The church contains tablets and windows commemorating gifts by benefactors. Its centenary was celebrated on the 15th December, 1957.

Close up view of Our Lady's Church and Presbytery - Circa 1920.
The presbytery has been demolished and rebuilt on the right hand side of the church.

Our Lady's Church is on the left of this walking day photograph with the Church Institute on the right. Tommy Halliwell is holding the guide rope – centre. The school superintendent Miah Southern is far left.

Close up view of Our Lady's Church Institute. The girl in front is Dorothy Southern, followed by the Reverend Senar, with John Ackers Wood – Headmaster of Haigh School – far left, and John Nelson – Lay Reader/Peoples' Warden near to the car.

Holy Communion Class at Our Lady's.
29th March, 1934.
Back Row: Mary Grady, Annie Grady, Mildred King, May Spencer, Margaret Duffy, Eileen Duffy.
Front Row: Ted Higham, Frank Ford, Bob Unsworth.

ASPULL METHODIST CHURCH

One day in 1990, I was returning from Wigan when I noticed that the Aspull Methodist Church was being demolished. I approached the site worker who allowed me to take photographs and I asked whether or not anything had come to light from beneath the foundation stones. The man was a little puzzled so I pointed out an inscribed stone, which he promptly dislodged and there lay an old broken soda glass bottle which contained an old Wigan Observer dated the 18th October 1879, a plan of public religious services of the Weslayan Methodists in the Wigan Circuit from October 26th, 1879 to January 24th 1880, a list of persons involved and an Old Victorian 'bun head' penny.

Over the ensuing days I photographed the progress of the demolition and subsequently, the rebuilding of the new church and a block of 32 flats on the old church site.

A selection of these photographs is included.

Aspull Methodist Church, 1990. Demolition has begun on the church. The Queen's Head Inn is to the left.

A foundation stone is situated below the arm of the track laying vehicle in use. The time capsule was below the stone.

Articles, from below the foundation stone.

Reverse of the Victorian penny recovered, showing the date 1877.

Copy of the Wigan Observer dated Saturday 18th October, 1879, which was inside the broken bottle.

Interior of the church.

Apart from the lack of windows, the church looks almost usable.

Building of flats on the site of the old church.

Rebuilding of Aspull Methodist Church.

Aspull Methodist Church on completion 1992.

WHELLEY METHODIST CHAPEL

Another Methodist Chapel to have disappeared is the Whelley Methodist Chapel, built in 1868. The site is presently occupied by a newly built private residence.

Close-up of Whelley Methodist Chapel.

Whelley Methodist Chapel is on the right of this photograph.

ST. ELIZABETH'S CHURCH, ASPULL

Consecrated on All Saints Day (November 1st) 1882, St Elizabeth's Church, Aspull, replaced the church of St. Margaret, Pennington Green. It was originally a Chapel of Ease for St David's Church, Haigh, but eventually assumed full status when a new parish was created. Pevsner records the date of building as 1876 by J Medland Taylor and Henry Taylor. The description reads:-

"Stock brick and red brick. No tower. W front with a typical Taylor motif: stepped-up lancet lights for the aisle W windows to follow the roof line of the aisles".

St. Elizabeth's Church Aspull. Circa 1920.

Interior of St. Elizabeth's Church, Aspull.
Circa 1920.

Reverend George F. Grundy, M.A., the second
Vicar at St. Elizabeth's Church, who succeeded
Reverend Robert Walmsley, M.A.

St. Elizabeth's Vicarage, 2000.

ST. MARGARET'S CHURCH, PENNINGTON GREEN, ASPULL

St. Margaret's Church and School, Pennington Green, Aspull. Circa 1910.

St. Margaret's was, in effect, a private chapel for Hindley Hall. Mr. Roger Leigh, M.P., of Hindley Hall, largely financed the building of St. Elizabeth's Church, Aspull, and the church school. A sum of £1,200 was also donated by the Earl of Crawford. The altar and a brass cross from St. Margaret's Church were transferred for use at St. Elizabeth's.

ST. STEPHEN'S CHURCH, WHELLEY

St. Stephen's Church, Whelley, 1914.

SCHOOLS

OUR LADY'S R.C. SCHOOL

Our Lady's R.C. School. Circa 1960.

St. David's Church choir in procession (1950). Our Lady's R.C. School is in the background to the right of this photograph. The school was subsequently demolished and a new one built on the opposite side of the road. John Pendlebury is the choirboy at the front. His family lived at Higher Highfield Farm, Haigh Road, Aspull.

Our Lady's School. Circa 1942

Pictured in Fancy Dress, from Left to Right, are:- Back Row: Kenneth Bowden, Kathleen Benson, Jim Whimsey, John Tierney, Bernard Gaskell, Kenny Hibbert, Tony Gaskell, Vince Durkin, Terrence Durkin, Brian Ranwell, Tony Derkin, ??.

Third Row: Eileen Grady (Smith), Pearl Taylor, Monica Duffy, Barbara Unsworth (Livesey), Molly Whittle, Doreen Traynor, Jean Relphs, Marion Whittle, Joanie Whittle, Marie Whimsey (Cottle), Sheila Durking, ??.

Second Row: Raymond Ramwell, ??, Ivy Pemberton, Rita Whittle, Rose Gaskell (Hyland), Helen Whittle, Sheila Hammer, Pauline Fishwick, ??, Yvonne Breckall, Josephine Unsworth, Edna Hilton, ??.

Front Row: Anthony Ramwell, ??, Kevin Dowd, ??, John Duffy, Jack Eastham, ??, Alan Seddon, Bill Grady, Kathleen Tindall.

Our Lady's School, Aspull. 1965.
Back Row (L to R): Elaine Rigby, Ann Gardener, Marie Gardener, Margaret McKeown, ??, Mary Unsworth, ??, Kathryn Hope, Una Houghton.
Middle Row: Vera Woosenham, Mary Aspinall, Julie Connor, Angela Bird, Janet Longshaw, Jean Riding, Ann Webber.
Front Row: Ann Lee, Janet Siney, Michelle Mulligan, Jeanette Roberts, Sarah How, ??, Maria Marcroft, Katherine Green, Pauline Sharrock, ??, Margaret Aspinall, Rita Moran, Catherine Connor.

Our Lady's School, Aspull. 1965
Back Row (L to R): ??, Christopher Halliwell, ? Houghton, John Unsworth, Peter Hennesey, John Moore, Christopher Cummings, John Makinson, Paul Roberts, ??, Sean Siney, Jimmy Critchley, John Bailey, Peter Holt.
Middle Row: Clifford Ashurst, Robert Halliwell, Peter Bunting, ??, Barry Guinette, Michael Grimes, Jimmy Turtington, Charles Briggs, Martin Moran, Denis Miller, Ian Verhaege, Danney Dewhurst, Anthony Dean, Paul Webbert, Keith Guinette, Kevin Duffy, Paul McNab.
Front Row: ??, James Hienke, Kevin Staziker, ??, Paul Phillips, Carl Bracegirdle, Martin Ashurst, Paul Kellet, Maria Marcroft, John Whistlecroft, ??, ??, Philip Unsworth, Steven Cottle, Steve Guinette, Simon Carey.

Our Lady's R.C. School. Circa 1970
At this stage some of the fabric of the building was giving concern. Some buttresswork is evident on the left.

The Bishop of Salford opened and dedicated the new Our Lady's School on the 7th December, 1976. Father Moriarty is on the left.

Our Lady's R.C. Primary School. 2000

The school is situated at the junction of Haigh Road with Holly Road. It was opened by the Bishop of Salford in 1976.

ASPULL METHODIST SCHOOL

A Methodist School was erected in 1879, which stood next to the church on Wigan Road.

On the stone tablet to the right are the words Wesleyan Schools and the date which is difficult to read but is believed to be 1879.

ST. ELIZABETH'S C. OF E. SCHOOL, ASPULL.

St. Elizabeth's Parish Hall, Bolton Road, Aspull. 2000.

Until 1982 this property was St. Elizabeth's C. of E. School, originally opened on the 12th August 1878

St. Elizabeth's C. of E. School. Circa 1970.
Reverend Donald Pankhurst of St. Elizabeth's Church, at the Christmas Fair,
opened by the Rose Queen, Joan Giffiths (far left).

St. Elizabeth's C. of E. School. Circa 1975.
Amongst the class are Gillian Whalley, Ann Griffiths, Liam Gough and Peter Ballard.
The form teacher is Mrs. Robillard (?).

ASPULL C. OF E. SCHOOL

Aapull C. of E, School was opened on the 27th January 1868. Aspull Endowed Grammar School built by subscription in 1770 was merged with the new school when it was completed. It became known as Aspull Moor Church School and finally Aspull C. of E. School.

Aspull C. of E. School stood near the Fingerpost at Aspull.
This photograph shows a class at the school about 1910.

Aspull C. of E. School. Circa 1950.
Back Row: 5th and 6th from the left Gerald Johnson and Stanley Wall, respectively.

Aspull C. of E. School. Circa 1930.
The persons in this photograph are all in fancy dress as though ready for a carnival or show.

Aspull C. of E. School. 1978.
Mrs. Henry with her class. On the back row, Michael Connor, Phillip Ivory, Anthony Taylor and Phillip Winstanley have been
identified, while on the front row (left to right) are Sarah Young, Diane Gilligan, Wendy Newsham, Michelle Stevens, Sharon Webb,
Andrea Aspinall, Susan Butterworth, Gina Banks, Deborah Winrow, Denise ?, Kathryn Winrow, and Carolyn Ellison.

ASPULL CHURCH PRIMARY SCHOOL

Aspull Church Primary School. 2000.
The school was built to accommodate pupils from St. Elizabeth's School, the C. of E. School, and Aspull Methodist School,
which all closed in October, 1982. It was built on the site of Aspull C. of E. School.

SCHOOL ATTENDANCE

School Attendance Certificate for Henry Marshall, Leyland Mill Farm, Haigh, in respect of Marleybone Public Elementary School for the years 1913 to 1920.

FARMING IN THE HAIGH AND ASPULL DISTRICTS

In the sales catalogue for Haigh Estate, published during 1943, is contained a list of 26 farms and various smallholdings which were, generally speaking, purchased by the tenants. (See Appendix 1.)

Farming was carried on in Haigh for many centuries under the old feudal system, evolved in Western Europe during the 8th and 9th centuries. Under this system the vassals were protected and maintained by their lords, usually through the granting of fiefs (property or fee). In return, the vassals were required to serve under the lord in time of war. This system was still in use at Haigh as late as the year 1785, after which time it was gradually phased out.

There are still many farms in and around Haigh and Aspull, a number of which are referred to below.

HIGHER HIGHFIELD FARM, ASPULL

Higher Highfield Farm. Circa 1950.
The datestone contained in the small square (top storey right) bears the date 1714. A Mission was established for Roman Catholics at Highfield and Jesuits were serving it in 1701. Father John Bennett was there until his death in 1751. Joan Pendlebury is seated on the window sill in this photograph.

John Pendlebury (Junior). Circa 1950.

Threshing machine at Higher Highfield Farm. Circa 1924.

Mr. H. Dawson is standing to the right. It was customary for farmers to hire the use of machinery because the cost of ownership was prohibitive. This threshing machine was hired from Mr. E.D. Robinson, who ran a forage and traction engine business in Chorley.

John Pendlebury with a short-horn bull at Higher Highfield Farm. Circa 1920.

Dorothy Pendlebury is standing back left with her sister Ida Mason, and her sister's children, Andrea and Paul B. Mason. Circa 1950.

John and Dorothy Pendlebury outside
Higher Highfield Farm with their niece
and nephew, Andrea and
Paul Barry Mason. Circa 1950.

John and Joan Pendlebury with
Paul Barry Mason. Circa 1955.

Higher Highfield Farm. 1995
Dorothy Pendlebury and her sister, Ida Mason, are in the doorway of the farmhouse.

Catherine (Cora) Pendlebury at Higher Highfield Farm.
Circa 1920.

GORSE'S FARM, ASPULL.

Gorse's Farm, Aspull. 1936.

John Pendlebury at Gorse's Farm.
Circa 1938.
His daughter, Joan, is on the horse.

PRESCOT'S FARM, ASPULL

Haigh School Walking Day. Circa 1920.
Prescot's Farm is on the right with the barn beside it.

WALKER'S LOWER FARM, ASPULL

Walker's Lower Farm. Circa 1950.

David Johnson of Walker's Lower Farm, remembered that his father, William Johnson, had to pick up this roller from Red Rock Railway station, when only nine years old, which was quite a responsibility for one so young. The roller is still at the farm. Photograph Circa 1915.

William Johnson with a friesian bull in the yard at Walker's Lower Farm. Circa 1950.

Mrs. Johnson with son, David, in the farmyard. Circa 1945.

A binder operated by William Johnson is drawn by three horses at Walker's Lower Farm. Circa 1935.

Haymaking at the farm. Circa 1940.

Barbara Johnson feeding the poultry at Walker's Lower Farm. Circa 1950.

Members of the Johnson family photographed at the farm.

PATCHCROFT FARM, HAIGH

Patchcroft Farm, Haigh is situated off Pennington Lane, Red Rock, near to Arley Brook.

HOME FARM, HAIGH ESTATE

Agnes Cliff is seated on the gatepost outside Patchcroft Farm.
Circa 1950.

Home Farm, Haigh Estate, 1999.
The stone tablet over the doorway of this building is very similar to the one at Tucker's Hill Farm. Beneath a coronet are the initials E.C.B. (Earl of Crawford and Balcarres) and the date 1867.

TUCKER'S HILL FARM, HAIGH

Tucker's Hill Farm, Haigh, 2000.
Above the hayloft is a tablet with a coronet, the initials E.B.
(Earl Balcarres) and the date 1841.

Members of the Marsden family from Tucker's Hill Farm, Haigh, ploughing land near the Haigh/Blackrod boundary. Circa 1930.
(Courtesy of the Bolton Evening News).

WILLOUGHBY FARM, HAIGH

Willoughby Farm, Meadow Pit Lane, Haigh, 2000.
Meadow Pit stood next to the farm on the left. It was closed in May 1927.

A mineral railway ran past Meadow Pit and on towards Toddington. The track bed for the old railway line can be seen in the centre. 2000.

WHITTLE TAG FARM, HAIGH

Whittle Tag Farm, Red Rock Lane, Haigh, 2000.

ABBEY FARM

Abbey Farm, Arley, 2000.
The Leeds and Liverpool Canal is in the foreground.

ORMSTON'S FARM, WESTHOUGHTON

Ormston's Farm, Westhoughton. Circa 1910.
John Pendlebury of Higher Highfield Farm, Aspull is seated at the front of the cart.

John and Dorothy Pendlebury with their daughter Joan at Ormston's Farm. Circa 1940.

WALKER'S HIGHER FARM (GRUNDY HOUSE) ASPULL

Walker's Higher Farm, also known as Grundy House, was built in 1755, which is attested to by a datestone at the front of the property. It is a Grade II Listed Building. The farm is one of the few buildings which appear on the 1786 Yate's Map of Lancashire.

Walker's Higher Farm. Circa 1950
Mary Farrimond is standing in the doorway of the farm with her grandson Colin Winrow. The datestone is between the second and third storeys. The centre window on the upper floor has been bricked-up. This was often done to avoid paying window-tax which was levied on windows in houses between 1695 and 1851.

Doreen and Brian Winrow, with their grandmother Mary Farrimond. The farm can be seen on the right.
Circa 1950.

Walker's Higher Farm. June, 1949.
Left to Right: Colin Winrow, Keith Spence and Brian Winrow, in the fields with farm horse 'Laddie'.

Walter Winrow treats his two sons to a donkey ride in the farmyard. The animal was affectionately known as 'Tinker'.

A David Brown tractor at Walker's Higher Farm, 1948.
Thomas Farrimond is seated on the tractor proudly holding a large bottle of spirit won at the Moorgate Inn.
Also present are Mary Farrimond with James and Arthur Winrow.

Harvesting at the farm, August, 1947.
(Left to Right) Pictured are Mrs. Green, Keith Spence, Elizabeth Spence, Walter Winrow, Colin Winrow, Mary Winrow, Mary Farrimond and Brian Winrow.

Two views of Walker's Higher Farm during turnip-thinning, when the crop seedlings were thinned to ensure a strong, healthy yield.

Above:— Walter Winrow with his sons Brian and Colin. Mrs. Green was a widow who always assisted on the farm at these times. Irish labourers also used to visit the farms to offer assistance with this type of labour intensive job.

Right:— Walter Winrow with Brian and Colin.

In the farmyard are (left to right) Brian, Colin and Doreen Winrow, with Irene Makinson.

GIDLOW HALL FARM, ASPULL

Gidlow Hall Farm. Circa 1950.

Gidlow Hall, Aspull, a moated property; was probably erected by the Goodlaws of Ashpool, mentioned in inquisitions of 1534 and 1606. Thomas Goodlawe married Anne the daughter and heir of Thomas Gerard of Ince, who died in 1544. From 1898 until it was sold in 1993 the Griffiths family held possession of Gidlow Hall Farm.

Gidlow Hall Farm. Circa 1970.

FIRS FARM, ASPULL

Firs Farm, Aspull. Circa 1970.

LEYLAND MILL FARM.

Leyland Mill Lane. Circa 1890.
Members of the Marshall family
from Leyland Mill Farm lead the
horses which are obviously pulling
a heavily laden cart.

HAIGH SHOW

Both Haigh and Aspull have large tracts of agricultural land and competition has always been keen between farmers to achieve the best. Haigh Show was organised as a showcase for the farming community where they could compete in various classes for prestigious prizes. It was similar, in many respects, to the Royal Lancashire Show.

Organisation of the show was by committee and it was a singular honour to feature amongst the members, albeit a great deal of work was involved.

Decline in farming, following the Second World War, resulted in the Haigh Show being discontinued but it has been re-instated in recent years.

Competitors at Haigh Show. Circa 1950.
Gerald Johnson of Walker's Lower Farm is to the left of centre.

Haigh Show Committee. Circa 1950
John Marshall is on the extreme left, with William Johnson second from the right. Other members include Lol Hart, James Marsden, John Langford, John Irvine, Dick Hindley, Ben Sutcliffe and Amos Ogden.

Two heifers prepared for Haigh Show by the Johnson Brothers Harry and Gerald from Walker's Lower Farm, Aspull. Circa 1950.

HAIGH AND ASPULL BRASS BANDS

In common with many mining communities, Haigh and Aspull boasted a number of brass bands with some excellent musicians. Competition was fierce between north-west bandsmen and it was no mean feat to secure one of the coveted prizes.

Aspull Temperance Brass Band used to practice in a bandroom at the top of Stanley Road, Aspull. As the name implies members belonged to the Sons of Temperance Movement which had a strong following.

Haigh Prize Band contained members from neighbouring towns and villages, including Leigh and Blackrod. At one time the Birkett family comprised a large contingent among the bandsmen and the band was also referred to as Birkett's Band.

Aspull Temperance Brass Band. Circa 1915.

Haigh Prize Band, outside Our Lady's Church, Haigh, 1955.
Back Row (L-R): Vince Quayle, Arthur Birkett, Billy Birkett, Walter Ainscough, Billy Ainscough, Eric Birkett, Bill Gill, Sid Rainford, Brian Birkett, Tommy Birkett.
Middle Row (L-R): Ralph Johnson (Librarian), Gordon Pilkington, John Barlow, Alf Birkett, Lot Birkett, Tom Birkett, Jack Birkett, Harold Mather, Wilf Gill, Alf Rudd, (Asst. Librarian).
Front Row (L-R): Jimmy Ryding, Billy Birkett, John Turner, Charlie Hulse (Conductor), Hugh Owen (President), George Ainscough, Sammy Taylor.

Haigh Prize Band photographed near to St. John's Church, New Springs, 1959/60. The Band won many trophies, some of which are displayed on the drum. Conducting the band at this time was Mr. Harry Bentham.

CARNIVALS AND PROCESSIONS.

There was ever a special pride in being a part of, or just watching, carnivals and walking days. Here was an opportunity to dress-up, either in Sunday best or costume, uniform etc. Brass bands were a necessity at these times and stirring martial music always put a spring in one's step. Fortunately, the camera was in constant use to capture friends and neighbours proclaiming their faith or just enjoying themselves on these memorable days. A series of shots, mostly personal photographs, are included which, it is hoped, capture the spirit of the moment.

Haigh Walking Day. Circa 1910.
At this time New Springs walked with St. David's Church. The group is pictured on the Windmill Field at Haigh.

A horse and cart bedecked for a procession at Haigh. Circa 1910.
The photograph was taken at Walker's Higher Farm, Amy Hilton is on the cart.

Walking Day Saturday in Haigh Road. Circa 1910.

The vantage point from which this photograph was taken, showing Prescot's Farm, Haigh Road, on the right, was very popular. Circa 1920.

Mr. Robert Weaver (left) leads the mens' procession along Haigh Road. Harold Cleveland, Licensee of the Victoria Inn, Haigh Road, is second in line on the right. Circa 1950.

John Ackers Wood, Headmaster of St. David's School, Haigh is on the right.

Haigh Carnival Queen. 1948/49.
Joan Dawson (nee Pendlebury) at the Crowning Ceremony. Mr. Farrington, Headmaster of St. David's School, Haigh is on the left.

Haigh Carnival Queen in procession near the Finger Post at Aspull, 1948/49.

LOCAL LADIES IN PROCESSION ON HAIGH ROAD DURING THE 1950s.

Identified amongst those walking are, Mrs. Tickle, Mrs. Birchall, Mrs. Lily Dawson, Mrs. Emma Hibbert and Evelyn Southern – Licensee of the Balcarres Arms.

Left to Right are Mrs. E. Hibbert, Mrs. Emma Hibbert, Joan Pendlebury, Lily Dawson, Mrs. Frances Hill, Peggy McKenna and Hilda Eckersley.

Denise Hart, Kathleen Parr, and Joan Pendlebury, are amongst the walkers

Present are Mrs. Miller, Mrs. Lickys, Mrs. Sanderson, Mrs. Jolly, Mrs. Pendlebury, Mrs. Troughton and Mrs. Carter.

Scouts, Girl Guides and Brownies process along Bolton Road, Aspull. Circa 1955.

Local children on walking day followed by a brass band. Circa 1945, in Bolton Road, Aspull.

Reverend Senar with his churchwardens Fred Wood and Tom Farrington, in Bolton Road, Aspull. Circa 1950.

Members of the Church Lads' Brigade on parade in Haigh Road, Aspull. Circa 1955.

Mr. J. Sixsmith carries the Crucifix in this procession of witness, June, 1956.

Red Rock Sunday School members assembled near Butcherfield Row on Haigh Road. Circa 1960.

Girls from Red Rock Sunday School on Haigh Road. Circa 1960.

Bolton Road, Aspull. Circa 1955. The nissen-hut at Roger's farm, on the left, was used for storage during the Second World War.

Jane Dawson at the Rose Queen Festival at St. David's Haigh, 1983.
Amongst her retinue are Elizabeth Cockram, Kerry Togher, Julie Brown, Isabel Lee, and the Jones children.

The Leeds and Liverpool Canal.

On the 7th April, 1720, an Act of Parliament was passed for making the River Douglas navigable from Wigan to the River Ribble. It was intended that coals, cannel, stone, slate and other goods and merchandise, could be carried for onward transhipment by coasters (sailing vessels of the time) to the various markets in Dublin, Lancaster, etc.

In January, 1772, the Leeds and Liverpool Canal Company purchased 28 of the whole 36 shares of the Douglas Navigation. The main reason for this was that it gave the Leeds and Liverpool Canal Company control over the water supply for its canal. Following the completion of the new canal much of the old river navigation was no longer of use.

The last section of the Leeds and Liverpool Canal to be constructed was from Blackburn to Wigan. An agreement was reached with the Lancaster Canal Company that an eleven-mile section of their canal from Johnson's Hillock to Kirkless, (Top Lock, Wigan) could be used to facilitate the final link. This was confirmed by act of parliament on the 21st June, 1819.

With all due ceremony, the Leeds and Liverpool Canal was officially opened on Saturday, 19th October 1816. One of the company's barges, along with one belonging to the Union Company, set sail from Leeds to Liverpool. On passing Haigh Hall, Lord Balcarres saluted the procession with cannon fire, then joined the party for the descent of the locks, followed by a luncheon provided by Colonel Clayton.

The Leeds and Liverpool Canal provided a valuable artery for transporting goods to the available markets. It proved so useful to trade that the Wigan Coal and Iron Company established one of the largest boatyards at the top of Wigan Locks. A fleet of more than 70 boats was operated by the company, some of them exceeding 70 feet in length. The longest boats could not reach the yard. The Haigh yard also had three side slips, only one other company having a similar number. Equipment was also available to repair iron barges.

Anglers on the Leeds and Liverpool Canal in Haigh Plantations. Circa 1900.

Haigh Plantations are divided by the canal into the lower and upper sections.

In 1872 the Wigan Rowing Club was established. The boathouse was situated at Basin Lane, Haigh. Earl Balcarres was the president of the club and members were admitted after being proposed and seconded at a committee meeting and agreed to by a majority of the committee present. Subscriptions were: -

1st to 5th year	30/-
6th to 10th year	25/-
11th to 15th year	15/-
16th to 20th year	10/-

Life membership was conferred on members completing 21 years full membership.

A silver trophy exists, the 'McCLURE CHALLENGE CUP', which was competed for annually. The plinth on which the cup stands has shields inscribed with the winners from 1921 until 1936, which read as follows: -

1921/22/23	J. CATTERALL
1924	J. LEA
1925	W.T. WALSH
1926	H. PEACOCK
1927	H. PEACOCK
1928	E. LUPTON
1929/36	T. GALE

With the demise of canal transport following the advent of the railways the canal system generally fell into disuse. However, the upsurge of leisure pursuits in the late twentieth century saw a marked increase in use of the canals by pleasure craft and has led to renewed interest in their maintenance and preservation.

The McClure Challenge Trophy competed for by members of Wigan Rowing Club.

Haigh Boat House is on the extreme right of this photograph. 1906.

Close up view of Haigh Boat House. Circa 1900.
This winter view shows the basin iced over. Bye-Laws for the Wigan Rowing Club prohibited members from putting boats in the basin during icy conditions.

Haigh Bridge (Hall Lane Bridge). Circa 1910.

Arley Hall. Circa 1930.
Arley Hall is the headquarters of Wigan Golf Club, which was founded in 1899.
The property is moated and stands close to the Leeds and Liverpool Canal.

Moat Bridge, Arley. 1908.

Canal boat trip through Haigh, 30th May 1953, to celebrate the Coronation of Queen Elizabeth II.

Red Rock Bridge, Leeds and Liverpool Canal, 2000.

Pleasure craft on the Leeds and Liverpool Canal near to Red Rock Bridge, 2000.

This aqueduct carries the Leeds and Liverpool Canal over the old railway line running from Red Rock Station to Adlington White Bear Station.

RAILWAYS AROUND HAIGH AND ASPULL

Four railway companies, namely the Great Central, the Lancashire and Yorkshire & Lancs. Union Joint (comprising the London & North Western and the L&Y), the L&Y and the L&N.W, ran railway lines in and around the Haigh district. A plan of the lay out of the railway system early in the twentieth century is included below.

In addition to the main rail routes, a complex network of mineral railways serviced the many collieries, Haigh Brewery, Haigh Foundry, etc., and connected with the main line system.

Several railway stations existed including Whelley Station, Red Rock Station, Standish Station and the Boar's Head Station (all now closed). There was also a well known signal box at Haigh Junction.

With the opening of new collieries in the 1830's and 1840's, the Earl of Crawford and Balcarres incorporated a network of mineral railway lines to service the complex and access the main rail routes. Whilst it is uncertain whether or not the lines were initially of standard or narrow gauge, they were eventually made compatible as standard gauge to allow for running on the main lines.

At present there are few clues left of the existence of the old railway network. Portions of the track-bed can be made out and a number of bridges remain. The Viaduct and bridge carrying the lines from the split at Sennicar Lane northwards, seem incongruous in their present setting.

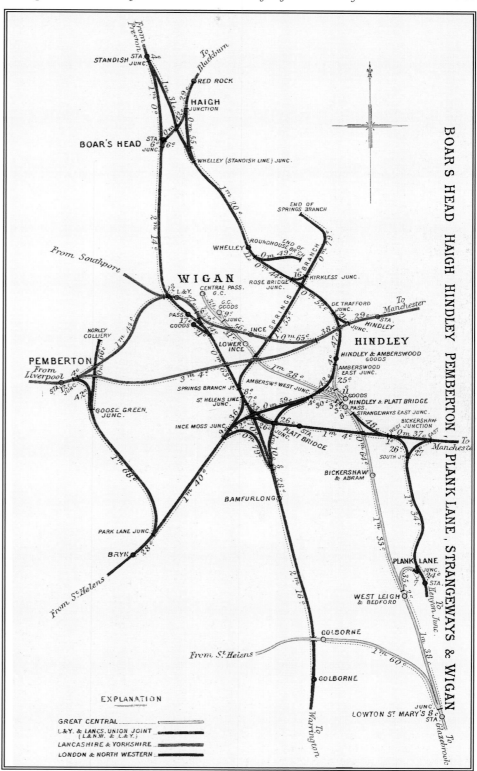

Railway routes around the Wigan area. Circa 1910

133

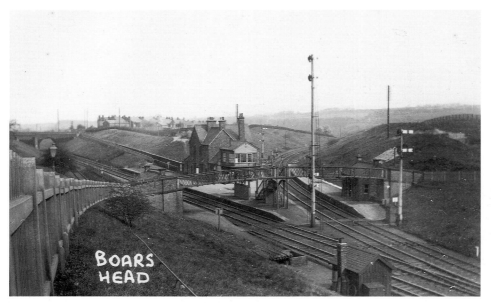

Boar's Head Railway Station. Circa 1930.

A view along the railway line through Haigh Plantations. Circa 1920.

Left: This interesting photograph shows the bridge over the old mineral railway line near Toddington, Haigh, the chimneys to which can be seen on the left. The bridge has since been demolished and the cutting for the railway line has been filled. Circa 1950.

Red Rock Railway Station. Circa 1920.

Mr. H. Dawson photographed in the 1920's in the fields near Meadow Pit. Coal waggons can be seen on the old mineral line in the background.

Remains of a railway viaduct which carries the main line form the Whelley Junction to Standish Railway Station, 2000.

View of the opposite side of the viaduct, 2000.
There is a notice warning of the danger from falling masonry and a request to notify the local authority.

Standish railway station circa. 1910. The station was closed in 1949.

Hindley railway station circa 1950.

WIGAN TRAMWAYS

The first trams ran in Wigan when the original line, from the Black Bull at Lamberhead Green, to Wallgate, was opened on the 31st July 1880. It had been decided that a narrow gauge of track would be used measuring 3' 6" as opposed to the standard width of 4' 8 $\frac{1}{2}$".

At the beginning of the twentieth century, Aspull Urban District Council requested an extension of the tramway from the terminus at New Springs to Aspull. This was agreed, provided that the council undertake to rebuild the steeply pitched canal bridge at New Springs. Consent was given to the request but Aspull U.D.C. failed to supply formal evidence for the House of Commons Committee on Private Bills and the provision for the extension was withdrawn.

Extending the tramway from New Springs to Aspull was finally sanctioned in 1905. Work commenced in October 1905 one condition being that a 3' 6" gauge was used but there was consent for a conversion to standard gauge at a later date.

Following inspection of the new route by Colonel Druitt, the extension to Aspull was officially opened on Thursday 12th April 1906. The turn-round terminus for the journey by tram was outside the Moorgate Inn at Aspull.

A series of experiments in 1922 resulted in the introduction of standard gauge track from Wigan to New Springs and the cessation of trams to Aspull. It was said that the line to Aspull was unprofitable and the tram service was replaced by buses.

PLANTATION GATES, WIGAN LANE, WIGAN.

Tram outside the Plantation Gates. Circa 1920.

A Dick Kerr double-decked tram with top cover, No. 18, at the terminus in Scot Lane, Aspull. Circa 1910.

Stanley Lane, Aspull, is in the background of this walking day photograph with the Moorgate Inn just visible behind the banner. The poles were part of the Lancashire Electric Power Company's low voltage distribution network. On the extreme left can be seen the mineral railway line. Circa 1910.

Moorgate Inn, Scot Lane, Aspull, 2000.

INDUSTRY AND COMMERCE

Included at Appendix 3 is the entry from Kelly's Directory of Lancashire, 1924 edition which includes Aspull with Haigh and Pennington Green.

By far the largest industry in the Haigh and Aspull district was coal mining. To give some idea of scale of the industry one only needs to scan a list of the many collieries once in existence which include, Newfoundland Colliery, Park Pit, Patchcroft Pit, Peacock Pit, Roger Lane Pit, Rough Hey Pit, Stone Hey Pit, Swan Pit, Tag Pit, Tucker's Hill Pit, Wash Pit and William Pit, at Haigh: with New Wash Pit, Perry's Pit, Wall Hey Pit, Withington Hall Colliery, Woodshaw Pit, etc., etc., at Aspull.

Pit Brow Girls and Boys from Aspull. Circa 1910.

Commercial interests operating in the area include the many farms, some of which have already been mentioned, Haigh Brewery, also referred to separately, Innkeepers and beer-sellers, with many other diverse business interests ranging from Robert Eastham, wringing machine repairer of 16 Crown Street, New Springs, to Wigan Motor Bodies Limited, motor body makers, Mariebonne Works.

A cross selection of illustrations is included to demonstrate the wide variety of work and retail activity carried on in the area.

Aspull Moor No. 5 Pit. Circa 1910.
Robert Weaver is on the right of this group,
holding a mallet.

This photograph taken by T. Silcock of New
Springs, Aspull, also shows surface workers at
Aspull Moor No. 5 Pit. Robert Weaver is second
from the left holding a hammer.

Orange Lodge procession, Aspull. Circa 1900.
Aspull Moor No. 5 Pit is in the background of this interesting old photograph.

Haigh Road, Aspull. 2000.
The building on the left, next to the garage, was once used by Aspull Moor No. 5 Pit and the colliery stood behind.
It is presently a Youth Club.

Moss Pit Row Cottages. 2000.
These cottages were erected for employees at the nearby Moss Pit.

Wigan Coal and Iron Company, Wigan. Circa 1900.

Blacksmiths' Shop, Wigan Coal and Iron Company. Circa 1900.

Vehicle constructed by Wigan Motor Bodies Ltd, Mariebonne Works, Wigan.

145

ROBERT SOUTHWORTH

R. Southworth's works yard off Haigh Road, Lane Ends. Circa 1920.
Mr Bolton, aged 16 years, is on the left next to Mr Bob Southworth.

CULRAVEN GARAGE

Culraven Garage, Haigh Road, Haigh. 1960.
The garage was opened by Fred Wood of Culraven House, Haigh.

Rowland (Rowley) Hill, Proprietor, is with his dog and
Freddie Seddon. Circa 1965.

Kenneth Hill at the garage. Circa 1965.

Garage staff. Circa 1965.

Rowland (Rowley) Hill and Dick McKenna at Culraven Garage. Circa 1970.

Dick McKenna, forecourt attendant at Culraven Garage. Circa 1970.

When petrol was still affordable! – The garage forecourt. Circa 1970.

PUBLIC HOUSES

The Victoria, Haigh Road, Aspull. Circa 1995.

The New Inn, Aspull. 2000.

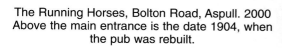

The Running Horses, Bolton Road, Aspull. 2000
Above the main entrance is the date 1904, when
the pub was rebuilt.

Hare and Hounds Hotel, Bolton Road, Aspull. 2000.
At the present time the pub is for lease.

THE CO-OP

Aspull Co-operative Stores are in the centre of this walking day photograph. Circa 1955.

ASPULL FINGERPOST SHOPS

Commercial properties on Scot Lane, Aspull. 2000

WAR AND REMEMBRANCE

The Roll of Honour for men from St. Elizabeth's Parish, Aspull, who served in the Great War (1914-1918), contains the names of 332 men, 30 of whom were killed in action (See Appendix 2 for full details). Many lives were also shattered by the effects of war and the suffering of local people was mirrored throughout the country in the other communities who would never see their loved ones again.

In Haigh, the Reverend Charles Henry James, M.A., vicar of St. David's Church, was particularly unfortunate in losing four sons. After the loss of three sons:-

1. George Sydney James, aged 22 years, a lieutenant in the '5th Manchester Regiment (T.F.), who was killed in action at Gallipoli, on the 4th June1915.

2. Francis Arthur James, M.A., James, aged 29 years, Captain in the 5th Manchester Regiment (T.F.), who died of wounds at Gallipoli, on the 18th September 1915.

3. Charles Edward James, aged 31 years, Corporal in the 13th Middlesex Regiment, who was killed in action in France, on the 28th September 1915.

the Baptistery at St. David's Church was adorned in memory of the three soldiers. The Right Reverend, The Lord Bishop of Liverpool carried out a service of dedication for the work on the 13th September 1916.

Subsequently, a fourth son, Sergeant Henry James, was also killed in action in France.

Two of Reverend James' sons appear on this 1914 photograph which shows officers of the 5th Battalion Manchester Regiment.

The four sons of Reverend Charles Henry James, M.A., Vicar of St. David's Church, Haigh and Aspull, who were killed in the Great War. 1914-18.

War Memorial, St. David's Church, Haigh. 2000.

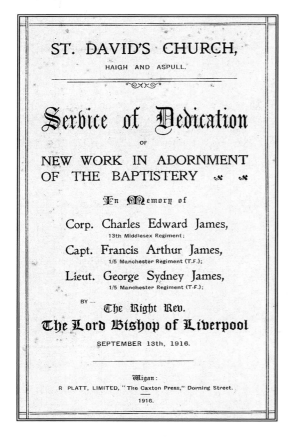

ST. DAVID'S CHURCH,

HAIGH AND ASPULL.

Service of Dedication

OF

NEW WORK IN ADORNMENT OF THE BAPTISTERY

In Memory of

Corp. Charles Edward James,
13th Middlesex Regiment:

Capt. Francis Arthur James,
1/5 Manchester Regiment (T.F.);

Lieut. George Sydney James,
1/5 Manchester Regiment (T.F.):

BY

The Right Rev.
The Lord Bishop of Liverpool

SEPTEMBER 13th, 1916.

Wigan:
R PLATT, LIMITED, "The Caxton Press," Dorning Street.
1916.

Description of the Work.

THE Walls up to a height of 5 feet 10 inches have been lined with oak panelling, and above with flecked Runcorn stone. The old window which was not in the centre of the wall has been taken out and a new window of three narrow lights put in, under which is an oak seat and panelling.

A floor of marble mosaic has been put down in the place of the former one of wood blocks.

A painted ceiling of wood has been put in place of the former sloping plaster ceiling, and an oak cover has been added to the Font.

On the South wall is a tablet bearing the following inscription:

To the Glory of God and in loving memory of

CHARLES EDWARD JAMES, Corporal 13th Middlesex Regiment, who was killed in action in France, on Sept. 28th, 1915, Aged 31 years;

FRANCIS ARTHUR JAMES, M.A., Camb., Captain 5th Manchester Regiment, T.F., who died of wounds in Gallipoli, Sept. 18th, 1915, Aged 29 years;

GEORGE SYDNEY JAMES, Lieut. 5th Manchester Regiment, T.F., who was killed in action in Gallipoli, June 4th, 1915, Aged 22 years; Sons of the Vicar of this Parish, the adornment of this Baptistery is dedicated.

They loved not their lives unto the death.

TABLETS IN THE BAPTISTERY AT ST. DAVID'S CHURCH, HAIGH.

Reverend James adorned the Baptistery at St. David's Church in memory of three sons killed in the First World War, during 1915.

A fourth son was reported missing but known to have been killed in action on the 18th August, 1916. This further tablet was added in commemoration.

Aspull and Haigh War Memorial, 2000.

HAIGH and ASPULL

Peace :: :: Celebrations.

SATURDAY,
19th JULY, 1919.

Programme

PROGRAMME.

THE SCHOLARS of the various Schools will assemble in their own school buildings at the time appointed by the teachers of each school.

Mr. Wm. BROADHURST will marshall the Procession, assisted by Mr. Hy. GIBSON.

2-0 P.M.—The Aspull Temperance Brass Band will start from Lane Ends, Haigh, accompanied by teachers and scholars from Haigh, Red Rock, and Our Lady's schools.

2-0 P.M.—The Haigh Band will start from Cale Lane end, New Springs, accompanied by teachers and scholars from New Springs schools, marshalled in their proper order (SIX ABREAST) by the respective sergeant-majors from each school. .

3-0 P.M.—The Teachers and Scholars will meet at the Finger Post, where the two Bands will play the National Anthem.

3-15 P.M.—The United Procession of the Teachers and Scholars, Haigh Parish Council, Aspull Urban District Council, Peace Celebrations Committee, and the Inhabitants of both townships (SIX ABREAST) will leave for the WINDMILL FIELD, Haigh, in the following order :—

1. Church Lads' Brigade.
2. Sailors, Soldiers and Airmen (discharged, de-mobilised, or at present serving).
3. Haigh School.
4. Red Rock School.
5. St. John the Baptist School.
6. Haigh Band.
7. Aspull New School.
8. St. Elizabeth's School.
9. Christ Church Mission.
10. Our Lady's School.
11. Holy Family School.
12. Aspull Temperance Brass Band.
13. Wesleyan Methodist School, Finger Post, Aspull.
14. Wesleyan Methodist School, Cale Lane, New Springs.
15. Independent Methodist School, Dicconson Lane.
16. Independent Methodist School, New Springs.
17. Primitive Methodist School, Scot Lane, Aspull.
18. Primitive Methodist School, New Springs.
19. The Lurries with Infants will follow, commencing with New Springs Council School.
20. The Members of the Haigh Parish Council and the Aspull Urban District Council, accompanied by the Officers of the respective bodies.
21. The Peace Celebrations Committee.
22. The Inhabitants of the two townships.

On arriving at the WINDMILL FIELD, the Bands will take up a central position, the teachers and scholars will form into position, when the National Anthem (*as printed on back*) will be sung, under the conductorship of Mr. SAMUEL BIRKETT (Haigh Bandmaster).

4-30 P.M.—The Bun and Sweet Stalls will be open, when each scholar will be served with a bun, cake, and a packet of sweets, on presenting the *Red* Ticket.

4-30 P.M.—The Ginger Beer Stalls will be open, when each scholar will be served with half-a-pint of ginger beer, on presenting the Ticket marked "Ginger Beer."

NOTE.—The scholars will not be required to bring their own mugs. Mugs will be provided by the Committee, WHICH MUST NOT BE TAKEN AWAY

5-0 P.M.—Older scholars will be provided with a meat pie, on presenting the *Blue* Ticket.

NOTE.—In consequence of the danger arising from broken bottles NO BOTTLED MINERAL WATERS WILL BE ALLOWED TO BE SOLD, nor any alcoholic drink.

The Bands will play Selections of Music during the evening.

Anyone desirous of entering Haigh Hall Park will be at liberty to do so ; Lord Crawford has kindly consented to leave same open for the occasion.

It is most sincerely hoped that everyone will assist the Committee in keeping order and in protecting the trees, shrubs and fences in the field and park from damage, and in seeing that nothing occurs to spoil the enjoyment of the day.

R. ARMOUR, *Hon. Secy.*

"*God Save the King.*"

ASPULL AND HAIGH WAR MEMORIAL.

CEREMONY OF UNVEILING

by Lieut.-General SIR R. K. H. BUTLER, K.C.B., K.C.M.G.,
General Officer Commanding Western Command,   and

DEDICATION by the REV. C. H. JAMES, M.A.,

On Sunday, September 6th, 1925, at 3 o'clock.

THE WAR MEMORIAL COMMITTEE invite

The Staff and Scholars of Haigh S.S.

to take part in the PROCESSION which will be formed at the NEW SCHOOL,
BOLTON ROAD, AT 2-30, in connection with the above-named ceremony.

Aspull and Haigh War Memorial, which stands at the Fingerpost, Aspull, was unveiled by Lieut. General Sir R.K.H. Butler, K.C.B., K.C.M.G., General Officer Commanding Western Command, at 3pm on Sunday, 6th September 1925. The dedication was by Reverend C.H. James, M.A., of St. David's Church, Haigh.

ST. DAVID'S CHURCH,

HAIGH AND ASPULL.

Dec. 7th, 1920.

THE PARISH CHURCH WAR MEMORIAL.

We beg to inform you that this Memorial, to which you so kindly subscribed will be dedicated by the Lord Bishop of Liverpool, on the evening of Monday, December 13th, at 8 o'clock, when we trust that you may be able to be present.

THE WARDENS.

MEN FROM HAIGH KILLED IN THE 1914-18 WAR

Albert Airey	William Hulme
James Balfour	Charles E James
James Bibby	Francis A James
Henry Cartwright	Henry James
Albert Crompton	G. Sidney James
Thomas Croston	Joseph Miller
Alexander Cush	Robert J. McCartney
Sidney K Haddock	Herbert Pickup
Vernon Holland	James Prescott
Bertie Hocking	John E. Young

St. Elizabeth's Church, Aspull.
War Memorial to those men who fell in the
Great War 1914-1918.

During the Second World War an American B.24 Liberator Bomber crashed in fields off Hall Lane, Hindley. Mr Hugh Heyes, who now lives in Salisbury, Massachusetts, U.S.A., was ten years old at the time of the crash and lived in Aspull. He has since pieced together details of the crash which are briefly as follows:-

At 7 p.m. on Friday, 17th August 1943, a B 24 H Liberator Bomber, number 42-7467, attached to the 392 Bomber Group, Wendling Station, took off from Burtonwood Air Depot. The plane was piloted by Richard L. Hester, 1st Lieutenant (Serial No. 0-427334), with William H Cambell, 2nd Lieutenant (Serial No. 0-659244) as co-pilot and Bernard H Froelich, 2nd lieutenant (Serial No. 0-856589 as Operation Gunner.

After circling the airfield twice, the plane climbed to a height of 8,000 feet, then proceeded northwards. Lieutenant Campbell noticed soon after take-off that No. 3 propeller was running fast and he began to make the necessary adjustments to correct the situation but without success. Soon all the propeller controls were failing to respond and the aircraft became violently unstable rolling from one side to the other. The bomber quickly lost altitude and both pilot and co-pilot fought desperately to regain control.

Descending to a height of 4,000 feet, the pilot called for parachutes and headed the aircraft towards the open sea. There was almost a full load of fuel on board which would cause a tremendous fireball if the aircraft crashed and would be disastrous in a populous area. However, at a height of 1,000 feet sufficient control had been gained to crash-land the plane in relative safety.

Eventually the aircraft hit the ground at 115 miles per hour. The port wing was at an angle of five degrees at the time of impact and the bomber bounced three times before breaking apart and coming to rest only feet from Hall Lane, Aspull. The pilot and co-pilot baled out of the side windows and it is presumed that Lieutenant Froelich did likewise.

It was then 7.20 p.m., only twenty minutes since the aeroplane left Burtonwood. At this time Thomas William Darlington, aged 38 years, of Bradshaw Hall Farm, was working on a binder at the farm, while his son, Thomas Darlington, aged 15 years, drove the tractor. They saw the bomber come down and immediately went to help. The air-crew were outside the plane, two were conscious and one was lying on the grass unconscious. A fire had started in the wreckage so assistance was given to move the unconscious airman a safe distance away.

In a very short time, the local police, Doctor Cooke and Fire Service Units from Wigan, Hindley and Westhoughton, were in attendance. Wigan Borough Police Ambulance personnel took the seriously injured Lieutenants Froelich and Hester to Wigan Infirmary. Lieutenant Cambell had sustained only bruising to the left arm and stayed to assist the emergency services. Sadly, Lieutenant Froelich died on his way to hospital.

A police guard was put on the crashed aircraft to deter souvenir hunters and within two days a party of American servicemen attended the crash site and cleared the area. They were accommodated at Pennington Hall Farm during their stay.

Although there is local knowledge of the crash, details were only sketchy and it is thanks to Mr Heyes that the story can now be properly related.

Pennington Hall Farm, Pennington Green, Aspull. 2000.
The brickwork on the left contains the date 1653.

Fields behind Pennington Hall Farm in which the American Liberator Bomber, No. 42-7467, crash landed on Friday 17th August 1943. St. Elizabeth's Church is visible on the horizon far right. The present occupant of the farm, John Johnston, has often turned up pieces of aluminium from the aircraft when ploughing.

Party in Aspull to celebrate Victory in Europe Day, 1945. This was held behind the Gerard Arms on a piece of land known locally as the 'Bank'.

Aspull Urban District Council.

The Ceremony of
Unveiling and Dedication
of the
Tablet

CONTAINING THE NAMES OF ALL ASPULL
SERVICEMEN WHO GAVE THEIR LIVES DURING
THE WAR OF 1939 - 1945.

Sunday, 24th July, 1949, at 3·0 p.m.

READING OF NAMES.

The names of the before-mentioned persons will then be read by the Clerk of the Aspull Urban District Council, Mr. Peter Ryder, as follows:—

WALTER BARTON	THOMAS PILKINGTON
JOHN BIMSON	THOMAS RAINFORD
JAMES EDWARD BROOMHEAD	WILLIAM RALPHS
JOHN WILLIAM BROOMHEAD	NATHAN ROBINSON
WILLIAM CAINE	JOSEPH SEDDON
THOMAS CASSIDY	LESLIE SEDDON
GEORGE COLLIER	WILLIAM SETTLE
LAMBERT CROMPTON	ALBERT SOUTHERN
WILLIAM GREEN	JOSEPH SIMM
JOHN GREGORY	ROBERT HENRY SUTCH
SIDNEY HOLCROFT HADDOCK	JOSEPH TICKLE
JOHN HALL	ALBERT TIERNEY
KENNETH HARRISON	WILLIAM WALMSLEY
WILLIAM HEYES	JOSEPH WARD
JOHN HUGHES	WILLIAM WEBBER
WILLIAM INGHAM	WILFRED WILLIAMS
JOHN INGRAM	ERNEST WINSTANLEY
ERNEST ISHERWOOD	JOHN WOOD
HARRY MAKINSON	CLIFFORD WOODS
WILLIAM MORGAN	WILLIAM YOUNG

THE DEDICATION.

The Vicar of St. Elizabeth's, Aspull, will dedicate the new inscription, saying:

" To the Glory of God, and in thankful memory of those from Aspull Who gave their lives in the last Great War, we dedicate this inscription in the name of the Father and of the Son and of the Holy Ghost. Amen."

Wreaths will be laid in the following order:

1. Aspull British Legion.
2. New Springs British Legion.
3. Chairman of the Aspull U.D.C. (Councillor John Higham, J.P.)
4. Relatives, Churches, Chapels and other Bodies.

THE UNVEILING.

The Tablet containing the names of those who fell in the war of 1939-1945 will be unveiled by the Chairman of the Aspull Urban District Council (Councillor John Higham, J.P.), with the following words:

" In thankful Remembrance of those of this township who went forth to the war and did not return, I unveil this Tablet. God proved them and found them worthy for Himself."

The Unveiling of the Tablet containing names of the Fallen will be performed by the *Chairman of the Aspull Urban District Council (Councillor John Higham, J.P.)* and the Dedication Service will be conducted by :—

The Vicar of St. Elizabeth's, Aspull.
      (*The Rev. E. O. Beard*),
assisted by . . .
The Vicar of St. David's, Haigh and Aspull
      (*The Rev. H. Senar*),
and *The Priest-in-Charge of St. John the Baptist's, New Springs, (The Rev. S. Singer).*

Councillor Joshua Mawdsley will act as Chief Marshal at the War Memorial Site.

Unveiling and Dedication of a tablet to those who gave their lives in the 1939-1945 War, 26th July 1949.

MEN OF HAIGH KILLED DURING THE 1939-45 WAR

Roy Armer

John Astley

George Collier

Alfred Crompton

Sidney Fairhurst

William Heyes

Leslie Hill

James Makinson

Thomas Pilkington

Arthur Postlethwaite

Nathan Robinson

Joseph Seddon

Claud Sherriff

William Webber
Joseph Whitter

Aspull St. Elizabeth's Choir assembled at the Cenotaph, circa 1960. Far right is Mr Jack Peet, organist and choirmaster.

MISCELLANY

There are many properties in the Haigh and Aspull District each of which has its own special history deserving of individual attention. However, while it is beyond the scope of the work to include every single property, a random selection appear below.

BOAR'S HEAD HOTEL

Boar's Head Hotel, Wigan Road, Standish. 1919

PENDLEBURY COTTAGES, HAIGH

Pendlebury Cottages. Circa 1910.
The family standing at the door with a babe-in-arms are believed to be the Prescotts.

TODDINGTON

Toddington, Haigh. 1904.
On the sale of Haigh Estate in 1943, the tenant of Toddington was A. D. Millard. The house and outbuildings are built of part stone, part brick with slate roofs. J. & J. Pendlebury presently trade as Toddington Farms, dealing in Pedigree and Commercial Charolais & Limousin, from the property.

Bridge over the mineral railway line near Toddington, with the pumping station on the left. 1950.

View from Toddington looking towards Tucker's Hill Farm. Toddington Delph is centre right. Circa 1950.

Duke's Row, Aspull.

INTERESTING ASSOCIATION OF THE HOUSE OF HAIGH.

J. Blackburn.

Duke's-row, Aspull, which is illustrated above, has an interesting history. The houses were built about 1754, and where possible stone was the material used, all the stone being hewn from a local quarry. Even the stairs are of stone, while the beams are of oak. Each house has only one exit —the front door. In one house three generations live at present, while in another four generations have been born, three still residing in this particular house. At one end of the row is a stone effigy of a man's head jutting up from the spouts, and this is known locally as "the Duke of Montrose."

Enquiries made by an "Observer" representative in connection with the local name of this effigy, revealed what appears to be an interesting association with an illustrious member of the House of Haigh, long since dead.

In Burke's Peerage, it is set forth how David, 5th Earl of Crawford, Lord of Lindsay, who was born in 1440 and succeeded to the Earldom in 1453, "attained a grandeur and magnificence which constitutes him the greatest personage of this eminent family. He was created 1488 and 1489, Duke of Montrose, which dignity was not assumed by his successors, but is claimed by his representative." This 5th Earl of Crawford was created Duke of Montrose by James III. of Scotland on account of his services, having been "for twenty years employed in almost every embassy that took place between England and his native country," for which "he was indeed well qualified, being princely in all his dealings." Shortly after conferment of the title James III. was slain at the Battle of Sauchieburn, and Parliament passed an Act known as the Rescissory Act annulling all the dignities made by James III. during the last eight months of his lifetime. In the following September, however, the Dukedom of Montrose was re-conferred upon the 5th Earl of Crawford, but owing to a curious wording of the Latin patent the grant was held to be a life grant only, and accordingly was not assumed by his successors. Subsequent Earls of Crawford have, however, it is stated, sought to maintain their right to the title, without pursuing it to any definite conclusion.

The property here illustrated is owned by the Haigh Eestate.

Duke's Row, Aspull. 2000.
In the 19th century the cottages were known as Fothershaw Row.

THE VON BLUCHER (ALEXANDRA), WHELLEY

The Grand Wedding, Whelley, Wigan. Circa 1910.
This is thought to be a carnival float enacting a 'society' wedding judging by the clown holding a bottle of champagne. It was customary to stop at the 'Von Blucher' for refreshments. During the First World War the 'Von Blucher' was renamed the 'Alexandra' because the former name had German connections.

Gerrard Arms, Bolton Road, Aspull. Circa 1950.
Pictured (left to right) are Cyril Westhead, Len Baron, John Westhead, Colin Heyes, Hugh Heyes, Sam Westhead and Harold Crompton

MARLEYBONE POST OFFICE

Marleybone Post Office, Wigan. 1912
The post office is the white building on the left and adjoining a row of stone cottages. W.H. Stevenson's name appears above the post office window. The area was referred to as Mariebonne Village, but Marleybone is now accepted.

CHERRY GARDEN HOTEL

Cherry Garden Hotel. 1905.
James Norris was the licensee at the time that this photograph was taken. Brierley and Howarth of Hindley are making a delivery of drink in the old stone flagons which were often utilised as hot water bottles.

MAYFLOWER COTTAGES

Mayflower Cottages. Circa 1900.
On the back of this postcard the small girl on the left is referred to as 'Florrie'. 'Mayflower' was the name of the ship which carried the Pilgrim Fathers to America in 1620. Their leader was Captain Myles Standish.

STANDISH BLEACHWORKS

Standish Bleachworks, Chorley Road, Worthington. 1906.
A colliery is visible, back centre, which is probably Victoria Colliery.

NOTES AND JOTTINGS

FOXES AND HEDGEHOGS
In 1532, during the reign of Henry VIII, it was enacted that each parish should provide itself with a net for the destruction of "rooks, crows and choughs, and in 1566, during the reign of Elizabeth I, the Act was extended to include many other birds and a range of animals such as foxes, otters, polecats, hedgehogs and moles

During the seventeenth century, Aspull, Haigh, Winstanley and Billinge, seem to have been infested with foxes and hedgehogs. One shilling (5 pence) was paid for a fox head and two pence (1 pence) for a hedgehog. In the Churchwarden's accounts for 1676, money was paid for 264 fox heads, whilst in 1677 disbursements for hedgehogs almost fill the accounts.

The practice ceased in the early eighteenth century.

DEATH AT BRYNNE HALL
Mr Peter Bradshaw, the Popish priest at Brynne Hall, was this day (8th March 1675) interred at Wigan. He was uncle to Sir Roger Bradshaigh of Haigh.

TRADE AND INDUSTRY
James Winstanley of Haigh is the subject of an entry in the Wigan Court Leet for Michaelmas (12th October) 1700, for furnishing a 'dyall' for the Town Hall and setting up a new 'dyall' on the most convenient part of the church. He is not described as a clockmaker but as a burgess of Haigh. It seems that the 'dyalls' provided were sundials, provided at Mr Winstanley's own expense and he was, as a result, elected a burgess. Wigan Church had a clock and two sundials at this time. Sundials were necessary in those days to keep the clocks to time.

BEN HIBBERT
Ben Hibbert was confined to a bath chair following an accident in his youth but this did not prevent him getting around the district. He was a familiar figure in the area and the poem, reproduced opposite, was penned by him. It is a particularly poignant ode considering the difficulties of Ben's life.

Ben Hibbert in his 'wheelchair' watches a procession pass by.

I love to go to Meadow Pit
By way of Copperas Lane
A long way round I must admit
But all the more to gain.

Leave smell of ale and kindly friends,
The darts and dominoes,
The rugby game that never ends
In't Top, or in Owd Joe's.

Between St. David's Church and school
The road winds down the hill,
Where sheep just graze so safe and cool
Beside the old windmill.

The green and yellow meadowland,
The overhanging trees,
Now more of god I understand,
And every bird agrees.

Save for a bark, or a lamb's wee cry,
Peace reigns around Home Farm,
Though tractor trails I can't deny,
There's still an old world charm.

The road then winds round to the right,
Unless you care to call
To where the meek without a fight
Have won the lordly Hall.

Could men of Haigh, to such extent,
Have sinned that they deserved
The shameful stocks as punishment
Which now are here preserved?.

Below lies Wigan in the vale,
Long famous for her toil,
As witnessed by those hills of shale
And towers as black as oil.

Past old Haigh school and there's the gate,
In line the traffic speeds
From East to West as if they're late
But my way slower leads.

Then rest a while near Whittle Tag
Before the final bend,
And mingle with an old man's shag
A smoke of milder blend.

Here Blackpool Tower and Lakeland Hills
The Ribble out to sea
If blessed with sight, and weather wills,
Are there for all to see.

St Wilfred's bells and Catherine's ring
A joyful tune they play,
Their chimes at Evensong will sing
The ending of the day.

Composed by Ben Hibbert.

APPENDIX 1
Details of the auction of properties on Haigh Estate 1943

BY ORDER OF THE TRUSTEES.

TO BE SOLD BY AUCTION BY

BOULT, SON & MAPLES

on FRIDAY, the 21st day of May, 1943,

AS TO LOTS 1 TO 36 COMMENCING AT 12 p.m.
AS TO LOTS 38 TO 87 COMMENCING AT 2-15 p.m.

AT THE

CORPORATION BATHS CAFE, MILLGATE, WIGAN.

(Unless previously disposed of by private treaty)
Subject to the Conditions of Sale.

In the following or such Lots as may be determined at the time of the Auction.

The Outlying Portion of the HAIGH ESTATE, WIGAN.

TOTAL AREA 1616 ACRES OR THEREABOUTS.

The Property briefly described comprises :—

26 Farms, Various Small Holdings, Cottages, Accommodation Lands, &c.

ALSO THE VERY ATTRACTIVE RESIDENCE KNOWN AS
" LONGHURST," HAIGH, LEYLAND MILLS and HAIGH FOUNDRY.

WELL SECURED GROUND RENTS TOGETHER WITH THE
FREEHOLD REVERSION.

SITUATE IN THE PARISHES OF BLACKROD, ASPULL, ADLINGTON, HAIGH
AND WIGAN.

For further particulars apply to :—

The Solicitors :
PEACE & ELLIS,
18, King Street,
WIGAN.

The Auctioneers :
BOULT, SON & MAPLES,
5, Cook Street,
LIVERPOOL, 2.

WELL SECURED GROUND RENTS
Together with the Freehold Reversion.

Lot No.	Amount of Yearly Rent (£ s. d.)	Security	Gross (£ s. d.)	Rateable (£ s. d.)	Date of Lease
1	1 13 0	Payable out of Two Dwelling-houses Nos. 29-30 Scot Lane, Aspull.	27 0 0	16 0 0	Lease 999 years from 12th May, 1858.
2	0 10 0	Payable out of Part of the Roman Catholic Day School, Haigh Road, Aspull.	—	—	Lease 999 years from 12th May, 1861.
3	4 2 8	Payable out of House North Side of Higher Lane, Part of Crawford Villa, Aspull.	30 0 0	22 0 0	Lease 999 years from 12th May, 1881.
4	2 9 2	Payable out of Nos. 10-12 Scot Lane, Aspull.	33 10 0	20 0 0	Lease 999 years from 12th May, 1859.
5	3 2 2	Payable out of Nos. 20-24 Scot Lane, Aspull	52 10 0	31 0 0	Lease 999 years from 12th May, 1861.
6	2 0 0	Payable out of Nos. 53-54 Stanley Road, Aspull.	21 0 0	12 0 0	Lease 999 years from 20th October, 1815.
	0 5 0	Rent of Strip of Land at Rear of 53-54 Stanley Road, Aspull. Area approximately 326 square yards.	—	—	Tenure Freehold.
7	0 10 0	Payable out of Land adjoining 276 Wigan Road, Aspull.	—	—	Lease 999 years from 1st May, 1913.
8	3 0 8	Payable out of Post Office and Two Cottages adjacent 1-3 Scot Lane, Aspull	48 0 0	34 0 0	Lease 999 years from 12th May, 1857.
9	3 1 6	Payable out of 25-28 Scot Lane, Aspull.	44 0 0	28 0 0	Lease 999 years from 12th May, 1859.
10	4 0 0	Payable out of 34-36 Bolton Road, Aspull.	45 0 0	31 0 0	Lease 999 years from 1st May, 1908.
11	4 4 7	Payable out of Two Houses, " Bank Top," Higher Lane, Aspull.	38 0 0	23 0 0	Lease 999 years from 18th July, 1881.
12	3 2 2	Payable out of Nos. 31 to 34 Scot Lane, Aspull.	38 0 0	24 0 0	Lease 999 years from 12th May, 1856.
13	2 14 0	Payable out of Nos. 17-19 Scot Lane, Aspull.	39 10 0	25 0 0	Lease 999 years from 12th May, 1854.
14	0 15 7½	Payable out of Site of Nos. 58, 59, 60 Stanley Road, Aspull.	—	—	Lease 999 years from 23rd March, 1787.
15	3 0 0	Payable out of Nos. 13 to 16 Scot Lane, Aspull.	44 0 0	28 0 0	Lease 999 years from 12th May, 1854.
16	1 13 4	Payable out of Nos. 108 to 114 Scot Lane, Aspull.	38 0 0	24 0 0	Lease 999 years from 30th April, 1810.
17	3 10 0	Payable out of No. 80 Bolton Road, Aspull.	—	—	Lease 999 years from 12th May, 1900.

Lot No.	Amount of Yearly Rent (£ s. d.)	Security	Gross (£ s. d.)	Rateable (£ s. d.)	Date of Lease
18	4 12 8	Payable out of Nos. 4 to 9 Scot Lane, Aspull.	66 10 0	41 0 0	Lease 999 years from 12th May, 1869.
19	4 9 2	Payable out of Nos. 2 to 14 Bolton Road, Aspull.	60 0 0	36 0 0	Lease 999 years from 12th May, 1859.
20	1 16 8	Payable out of "The Bungalow," North of Moore Street, East side of Stanley Road, Aspull.	14 10 0	9 0 0	Lease 999 years from 13th July, 1861.
21	1 14 2	Payable out of 18-24 Wigan Road, Aspull.	38 0 0	22 0 0	Lease perpetual.
22	3 13 6½	Payable out of 72 and 72a Scot Lane, formerly Star Inn, Aspull.	31 0 0	18 0 0	Lease perpetual from 15th May, 1861.
23	2 7 0	Payable out of 50 to 52 Stanley Road, Aspull.	20 0 0	12 0 0	Lease perpetual from 25th July, 1863.
24	0 12 6	Payable out of what was the Site of Three Cottages, 66, 68 and 70 Wigan Road, Aspull.	—	—	Lease perpetual.
25	2 11 2	Payable out of 74-78 Scot Lane, Aspull.	39 10 0	21 0 0	Lease perpetual from 18th April, 1861.
26	0 10 0	Payable out of Land adjoining Mill Lane Cottages, Tuckers Hill Brow, Blackrod.	—	—	Lease 925 years from 1st November, 1908.
27	4 19 7	Payable out of Boatman's Arms (P.H.) West of Aberdeen Farm, Blackrod.	30 0 0	22 0 0	Lease 999 years from 12th May, 1866.
28	3 1 3	Payable out of "Riley" and "Sea View," Haigh Road, Haigh.	42 0 0	28 0 0	Lease 999 years from 12th May, 1875.
	0 11 0	Ditto and Gardens North and South side of "Riley" and "Sea View." Area approximately 720 square yards.	—	—	Lease 979 years from 12th May, 1895. Tenure Freehold.
29	2 7 6	Payable out of "Standish View," Arley Lane, Haigh.	22 0 0	15 0 0	Lease 999 years from 1st May, 1910.
30	4 0 8	Payable out of Bungalow "Mereside," Arley Lane, Haigh.	20 10 0	13 0 0	Lease 999 years from 1st November, 1934.
31	3 2 6	Payable out of 27 and 29 Poolstock Lane, Wigan.	38 0 0	24 0 0	Lease 999 years from 31st March, 1863.
32	3 18 6	Payable out of "Woodside," Hieland Road, Wigan.	32 0 0	24 0 0	Lease 999 years from 1st November, 1925.
33	2 5 0	Payable out of "The Mount," 215 Whelley, Wigan.	29 8 0	22 0 0	Lease 999 years from 1st May, 1913.
	0 14 0	Ditto	—	—	Lease 977½ years from 1st Nov., 1934.

Lot No.	Amount of Yearly Rent (£ s. d.)	Security	Gross (£ s. d.)	Rateable (£ s. d.)	Date of Lease
34	3 17 8	Payable out of 18 Hieland Road, Wigan.	28 0 0	21 0 0	Lease 999 years from 1st May, 1922.
35	0 5 0	Payable out of Day Schools, Whelley, Wigan.	—	—	Lease 990 years from 11th Nov., 1872.
	0 5 0				Lease 960 years from 11th Nov., 1902.
36	3 16 6	Payable out of Land at Rear of Cottages S.W. of Whelley Station, Wigan.	—	—	Lease 999 years from 12th Nov., 1876.

168

SUMMARY OF FARM LOTS, COTTAGES, Etc.

Lot No.	Description	Tenant	Rent £ s. d.	Area (Acres)
38	Crawshaw Hall Farm, Adlington	Mr. Wm. Heaps *1950*	58 10 0	49.491
39	Sharrock's Farm, Blackrod	Mr. H. Gibson	40 10 0	43.978
40	Goodmanfold Farm, Blackrod	Mr. James Marsden *4080* For Tip	180 0 0 7 0 0	143.833
41	Aberdeen Farm, Blackrod	Mr. P. Gregory	115 0 0	111.643
42	Crowshaw Farm, Blackrod	Mr. James Hodge *2300*	95 0 0	83.903
43	Rollinson House Farm, Blackrod	Mr. J. G. Halton *1500*	64 0 0	41.474
44	Pennington Fold Farm, Blackrod	Mr. Herbert Owen *1100*	30 0 0	19.413
45	Brown Fold Farm, Blackrod	Mrs. A. Owen (Reps.) *800*	31 10 0	24.182
46	Leigh's Tenement, Blackrod	Messrs. J. & E. Partington *1100*	44 0 0	25.165
47	Two Cottages, Chorley Road, Blackrod	Mrs. E. Mollison and another	22 0 0	.392
48	"Longhurst," Hall Lane, Haigh	Mr. C. E. Marsden	82 10 0	5.395
49	Wigan Golf Club Land, Haigh	Wigan Golf Club Trustees	17 10 0	11.827
50	Arley Cottage, Haigh	Mr. Francis Brown	12 0 0	.385
51	Land, Arley Lane, Haigh	Mrs. M. Taylor	5 0 0	1.620
52	Lower House Farm, Park House Farm and Two Cottages	Mr. T. Marshall *3500*	134 10 0	90.217
53	Worthington's Farm, Haigh	Mr. Elijah Collier *2750*	100 0 0	80.963
54	Fir Tree Farm, Haigh	Mr. E. Collier & Mrs. Whitter	72 0 0	70.724
55	Pennington's Farm, Haigh	Mrs. E. A. Walker (Exors.) *1265*	48 0 0	30.785
56	Patchcroft Farm, Haigh	Mr. A. Black	80 0 0	50.118
57	Hart's Farm, Haigh	Mr. Frank Taylor *2500*	94 0 0	68.035
58	Tucker's Hill Farm, Haigh	Mr. William Marsden *3700*	122 0 0	109.623
59	Willowby's Farm, Haigh	Mr. William Marsden *1900*	72 5 0	53.016
60	Nightingale's Farm, Haigh	Mr. John Kay *1000*	34 0 0	23.352
61	Freezeland Farm, Haigh	Mr. J. Murray	54 0 0	39.008
62	Two Semi-detached Cottages, Red Rock Lane, Haigh	Miss Ditchfield and another	25 7 6	.656
63	Glassbrook's Cottage, Red Rock Lane, Haigh	Mr. F. Hulbert	7 16 0	.269
64	Five Cottages, Leyland Mill Brow, Haigh	Mr. Wm. Lowe and others	81 0 8	.580
65	Packet House, New Springs Labour Club, Haigh	Labour Club Trustees	20 0 0	.265
66	Leyland Mills (Malt Extract), Haigh	Jeffrey's Miller & Co., Ltd.	110 0 0	2.978

Lot No.	Description	Tenant	Rent £ s. d.	Area (Acres)
67	Toddington, Aspull and Haigh	Mr. A. D. Milliard *400*	18 0 0	7.886
68	Gorse's Farm, Aspull	Mr. John Pendlebury *2500*	101 2 6	90.482
69	Higher Highfield Farm, Aspull	Mr. John Pendlebury *2400*	80 0 0	67.992
70	Stanley Nook Farm, Aspull	For Allotments Marsden Brothers *3900* For Allotments	2 0 0 101 0 0 1 17 6	87.063
71	Scot Lane Farm, Aspull	Mr. Pierce Croston *645*	33 10 0	14.793
72	Shepherd's Tenement, Aspull	Mr. Leonard Smith *750*	35 0 0	14.176
73	Walker's Higher Farm, Aspull	Mr. T. Hilton *1200* For Allotments *2200*	51 0 0 12 9 0	34.549
74	Walker's Lower Farm, Aspull	Mr. Henry Johnson	85 10 0	61.603
75	Accommodation Land and Allotments, Aspull	Mr. R. Holt *180*	6 0 0	4.850
76	Bradley House Farm, Aspull	Mr. John Pye and others *425* For Allotments	18 0 0 9 11 0	5.210
77	Traveller's Rest, Aspull	Mr. John E. Taylor *350*	24 10 0	.339
78	Two Cottages, 207 and 209 Wigan Road, Aspull	Mr. S. Harvey and another	29 9 4	—
79	Three Cottages, Mowpin Fold, Aspull	Mrs. Seddon and others	33 16 0	1.033
80	Building or Accommodation Land, Aspull	In hand	—	2.700
81	Accommodation Land, Whelley Road, Wigan	Exors. of Mr. H. Ramsdale	11 0 0	8.367
82	Snout Hey Field, Wigan	Mr. T. Marshall *420*	7 0 0	11.578
83	Haigh Foundry, Leyland Mill Lane, Wigan	Mr. R. Grundy	70 15 0	1.968
84	Four Cottages, 220-226 Whelley, Wigan	Mrs. Fielding and others For Hoardings	43 19 8 3 0 0	.080
85	Voses Field, Leyland Mill Lane, Wigan	Exors. C. Sawbridge *350*	17 0 0	7.540
86	Jolly Bottoms Field, Wigan	Mr. John King *450*	15 0 0	11.133
87	Four Cottages (Foundry Cottages) Wigan	Miss E. Metcalfe and others	55 9 4	.337

APPENDIX 2
First World War Roll of Honour St Elizabeth's Parish, Aspull

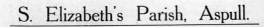

S. Elizabeth's Parish, Aspull.

1914   1918

Roll of Honour of the Men who served in the Great War.

AINSWORTH, JOHN, 606, Bolton Road (42104), R.A.M.C.

ASHCROFT, FRANK, 118, Bolton Road (40808), R.G.A. (3rd Siege Battery).

ARKWRIGHT, JAMES, 17, Bolton Road (Clogger).

ATHERTON, WM., Simm's Square, then Haigh Road (14556), Machine Gun Corps.

ATHERTON, SETH, Simm's Square (14555), 9th Cheshires.

ALPIN, WM., 79, Scot Lane (69909), R.G.A.

ALEXANDER, THOMAS, 69, Bolton Road 6th Border Regiment.

ASHTON, THOMAS, 352, Bolton Road (118559), 198th Labour Company.

ACTON, WM., 8, Simm's Square (4021), R.F.A.

ASHURST, WM., Young's Yard, 5th Manchesters.

ATHERTON, ERNEST, Stanley Road, then 9, Smith Street (258343), A.S.C. (Remounts).

†ASHTON, HARRY (R.I.P.), Mill Lane (243554), L.N. Lancs. (4/5 Battalion).

AINSCOUGH, WALTER, 384, Bolton Road (86952), 3rd L.N. Lancs. (R. Defence C.).

AINSCOUGH, HAROLD, 384, Bolton Road (64641), Lancashire Fusiliers.

AINSCOUGH, HY., 489, Bolton Road (31877), Grenadier Guards.

AINSCOUGH, SID., 489, Bolton Road (84000), Cheshires.

ALKER, NICHOLAS, 587, Bolton Road (65923), Lancashire Fusiliers.

†AUSTIN, JAMES (R.I.P.), Woodfield Street (13201), 12th Manchesters.

ASHTON, JOHN, 352, Bolton Road (266360), R.A.F.

BOND, RICHARD, 612, Bolton Road, nr. Gerrard Arms (24347), R.F.A.

BOND, WM., 612, Bolton Road, nr. Gerrard Arms (13948), Coldstreams.

BOND, JOHN, 67, Bolton Road (76304), R.F.A. (20th D.A.C.).

BALFOUR, STEPHEN, 279, Bolton Road (58690), R.E.

†BALFOUR, JAMES (R.I.P.), 2, Scot Lane (32057), R.A.M.C.

†BAKER, BENJ. (R.I.P.), Withington Lane (10526), L.N. Lancs.

BRAMWELL, JAMES, Leigh Street (10371), 14th King's Liverpool.

†BRYAN, FRED S. (Lieut.) (R.I.P.), Bell House, Hall Lane, 15th Middlesex.

BARON, EDWARD, 469, Bolton Road (53879), Royal Naval Division.

BAXTER, ABRAHAM, near Wingates Church (160963), R.G.A. (146th Siege B.).

BRAMWELL, ALBERT, 300, Bolton Road (18663), R.F.A.

BRINDLE, JOSEPH, Thorne Cottages, Bolton Road, Scottish Borderers.

BRINDLE, HENRY, Thorne Cottages, Bolton Road, K.R.R.

BOOTH, HENRY, 1, Mill Lane (21561), 1st Border Regiment.

†BENTLEY, WALTER (R.I.P.), 2, Heyes' Square.

BOND, WM., 253, Bolton Road, R.H.A.

BRAMWELL, WILFRED, 9, Mill Lane (207148), A.S.C.

BAILEY, ALFRED, 175, Scot Lane (47811), 3rd Yorks.

BROXTON, JAS. WM., 3, School Close (11969), 1st Border Regiment.

BARON, EDWARD, 534, Bolton Road (M. 20532), H.M.S. "Erebus."

BARON, JOSEPH, 534, Bolton Road, H.M.S.

BOND, EDWARD, 4, Mill Lane (54119), Lancashire Fusiliers.

BROWN, THOMAS, Bolton Road (12400), North Staffs.

BARKER, EDGAR (Lieut.), 471, Bolton Road, 14th King's Liverpool.

BARKER, H. J., 471, Bolton Road, (180132), A.S.C. (M.T.).

BARKER, THOMAS, 2, Holly Street, New Springs (53359), 397th Labour Company.

BROADSTOCK, HUMPHREY, Enton's Yard (54655), Lancashire Fusiliers.

BEARDSWORTH, JOHN, 63, Bolton Road (76844), Royal Welsh Fusiliers.

BIBBY, JOHN, 2, Heaton Street (186049), R.F.A.

BOND, MAT, 67, Bolton Road (110411), King's Liverpool (4th Battalion).

BERESFORD, JOHN, 14, Harold Street (67470), Lancashire Fusiliers.

BIRCHALL, THOMAS, 536, Bolton Road (116699), R.A.F.

BOARDMAN, HAROLD, 584, Bolton Road, R.A.F. (Cadet).

BIRD, W. F. (Lieut.), Bell House, Hall Lane, 1/2nd Lovat's Scouts.

BATES, WM., 66, Withington Lane (18727), 6th South Lancs.

†CARTWRIGHT, HY. (R.I.P.), 24, Bolton Road (257), King's Royal Rifles.

CARTWRIGHT, ERNEST, 24, Bolton Road (526954), R.R. Brigade (4th Batt.).

CLARK, PETER, 3, School Close (430094), R.E. (183rd Tunnelling Company).

CLARK, JOHN, 3, School Close (67469), Lancashire Fusiliers.

CROMPTON, WM., 5, Moss Pit Row (487280), 979th Labour Company.

CROMPTON, WM., 12, Hope Street (61032), Northumberland Fusiliers.

CROMPTON, CHAS. A., 12, Hope Street (22010), Grenadier Guards.

CROMPTON, LOT, 12, Hope Street (24348), R.F.A.

CROMPTON, LOT, Thorne Cottages (61255), Leicester Regiment.

CLEVELAND, JAMES, 257, Withington Lane.

COX, JNO. HY., Withington Lane, 1/5th Manchesters.

CHISNALL, HARRY, Ladies' Lane, Hindley, H.M.S. (R. Navy).

CLEMENTS, JOHN, 212, Withington Lane (88500), R.H.A.

†COLEMAN, JESSE (R.I.P.), 612, Bolton Road (21709), 2nd Scottish Borderers.

CAUSEY, HERB., 13, Duke's Row (52227), 80th Labour Company.

CRANK, EDWIN, 454, Bolton Road (28018), King's Shropshire Light Infantry.

COLLIER, RD. JOHNSON, 28, Scot Lane (171860), R.F.A.

†CROSTON, JNO. WM. (R.I.P.), 2, Old School Land (53988), 3rd Lancashire Fusiliers.

CANNON, JAMES, 2a, Harold Street (122188), R.F.C.

COLLIER, JEREMIAH, 8, Duke's Row.

CROSTON, HARRY, 55, Bolton Road (109457), King's Liverpool.

CHATTERLEY, JOHN, 11, Duke's Row (150366), R.G.A.

CAUSEY, WM., Shepherd's Farm, H.M.S. "Albion."

COLLIER, LEVI FRANCIS, 25, Scot Lane (305984), Tank Corps.

CHARNOCK, JOHN, 20, Woodfield Street (67470), 6th Dorsets.

CHRISTOPHER, JOHN, 154, Withington Lane (12604), A.S.C.

DUNDERDALE, RD. (M.M.), Bolton Road, R.F.A.

†DIXON, WM. (R.I.P.), Bolton Road, nr. Rushton's (260084), 5th Border.

DIXON, THOMAS, Bolton Road, nr. Rushton's, H.M.S. (Royal Navy).

DEAN, EDGAR RANKIN, 514, Bolton Road, R.G.A.

DICKINSON, ED., 14, Harold Street (15609), K.O. Lancs.

DILLON, CHAS. R., 218, Withington Lane (53919), 3rd Lancashire Fusiliers.

ECKERSLEY, WM., 67, Scot Lane (235300), 1/6th N. Staffs.

ECKERSLEY, BEN, 67, Scot Lane.

ECKERSLEY, JOHN, 6, Harold Street, H.M.S. (mine sweeper).

FRASER, WALT., 84, Scot Lane (80316), R.F.A.

FRASER, RD., 66, Scot Lane (201006), 1/5th Manchesters.

FIDDLER, ROBT., 33, Bolton Road (71281), Border Regiment.

FISHER, STANLEY, 67, Bolton Road (21706), Border Regiment.

FRANCE, WM., 497, Bolton Road (125370), R.E.

FLYNN, THOMAS, 61, Bolton Road (34005), L.N. Lancs.

FARRER, JAMES, 29, Stanley Road (25312), L.N. Lancs.

FEARNLEY, JOHN, 94, Scot Lane, H.M.S. "Lion."

FIDDLER, ED., 44, Reservoir Street (65339), Lancashire Fusiliers.

GREGORY, JOHN, 40, Scot Lane (43775), 5th Manchesters.

GREGORY, WALTER, 90, Scot Lane, R.F.A.

GREGORY, PETER, Mount Pleasant (8).

GREGORY, WM., Mount Pleasant (80315), R.F.A.

GILL, WM., 11, School Close (12325), 7th L.N. Lancs.

GLOVER, PERCY (Lieut.), Scot Lane, 41st Machine Gun Battery Company.

GRAHAM, JOHN, Woodfield Street.

GENT, WM. HY., 26, Bolton Road (76227), R.F.A.

GENT, COLIN, 26, Bolton Road.

GALE, JAMES, Withington Lane.

GREGORY, WM. GORDON, 97, Dicconson Lane (160984), Machine Gun Corps.

GREGORY, RALPH, 97, Dicconson Lane (19164), Coldstream Guards.

†GREEN, HORACE (R.I.P.), Dicconson Lane (16662), R.F.A.

GREGORY, HENRY, 598, Bolton Road (24487), R.F.A.

GERRARD, WALTER, 4, Pennington Green (3436), R.E.

GREGORY, GORDON, 530, Bolton Road (38729), 12th Nelson Infantry (N.Z.).

GRAY, EDWARD, 480, Bolton Road (22457), 5th K.O.R.L.I.

†GRAY, HENRY (R.I.P.), 480, Bolton Road (53982), 3rd Lancashire Fusiliers.

GOULDING, RD., 42, Reservoir Street (569274), 3rd R. Welsh Fusiliers.

GREGORY, RD., 61, Dicconson Lane (23738), Coldstream Guards.

GREGORY, JNO. PENNINGTON, Leeches Farm, H.M.S. (Crystal Palace).

GREGORY, NOAH, 596, Bolton Road (8081), R. Marine Light Infantry.

GERRARD, ALF., 7, Scot Lane, 1/5th Manchesters.

GERRARD, WM., 7, Scot Lane (380550), A.S.C. (Remounts).

GIBSON, HENRY, 16, Woodfield Street (67464), Lancashire Fusiliers.

GIBSON, FRANCIS, 41, Bolton Road (5149), 3rd Border Regiment.

†GREGORY, WM. (R.I.P.), 2, Hope Street (53981), Lancashire Fusiliers.

GRUNDY, ERNEST, 3, Mill Lane (71814), R. Welsh Fusiliers (Missing).

GREENACRE, CHAS. ALF., 18, Woodfield Street (200238), 1/5th Manchesters.

GREENWOOD, WM. (no address) (118115), R.F.A.

HOLDING, THOMAS, 26, Harold Street (88240), R.H.A.

HEYES, THOMAS, 4, Brinsop Street (29042), Leicesters.

HYLAND, FRED, 561, Bolton Road (17064), L.N. Lancs.

†HEAPS, JAMES (R.I.P.), 11, Bolton Road (27547), 18th Welsh Fusiliers.

†HOUGH, HAROLD (R.I.P.), 3, Ashworth Street (96847), 8th Border.

HEYES, ALBERT, 14, Bolton Road (200741), 5th Manchesters.

HIGHAM, ROBT., 5, Scot Lane (74634), R.F.A. (Driver).

HALL, THOMAS, 69, Bolton Road (241205), K.O.Y.L. Infantry.

HEYES, ALFRED, 3, Scot Lane (13607), R.F.A.

HEYES, WM. (Lieut.), 3, Scot Lane, R.E.

HEYES, JAMES, 3, Scot Lane (125857), R.A.M.C.

HOLLAND, WM., 1, Brownlow Fold (26133), 6th Manchesters.

HOPE, ROBERT (M.M.), 568, Bolton Road (117107), R.F.A.

HOPE, LEONARD, 568, Bolton Road (145807), Lancashire Fusiliers.

HORROCKS, JAS. HAMPSON, Dicconson Lane, R.A.F.

HARTLEY, EDWIN, 16, Bolton Road (24625), 11th Manchesters.

HEAPS, PETER, 11, Bolton Road (96370), 3rd R. Welsh Fusiliers.

HILL, SID, 14, Mayflower Cottage, Red Rock (971), York and Lancaster.

HUNT, WM., 104, Bolton Road (2171), Border Regiment.

HIGHAM, JAMES, 498, Bolton Road (118324), Lancashire Fusiliers.

HOLCROFT, THOMAS, 27, Bolton Road (V. 50299), R.A.M.C.

HOLCROFT, JAMES, 27, Bolton Road (266507), L.N. Lancs.

HOLCROFT, ROBT., 27, Bolton Road (M/Z. 4684), R. Navy.

HORNE, WM. HY., 575, Bolton Road (45237), Duke of Cornwall's.

HEYES, HEZEKIAH, 48, Scot Lane (263921), 2/5th King's Liverpool.

HUGHES, THOMAS, Ainscough's Farm (243038), L.N. Lancs. (Light Infantry).

HILLMAN, FRED, Ainscough's Farm, Cheshires.

†HILLMAN, GEO. (R.I.P.), Dicconson Lane, Machine Gun Corps.

HILLMAN, ALB., Ainscough's Farm, L.N. Lancs.

HIGHAM, JOHN, 30, Bolton Road (02484), 16th Worcesters.

HAYDOCK, SID, 28, Harold Street (2876), K.R.R. (Missing).

HEYES, ALEC, 57, Stanley Road (40429), 68th Labour Company.

HEYES, ALBERT, 57, Stanley Road (35357), 3rd Bedfords.

HEYES, ROBERT, 595, Bolton Road (305827), R.F.A.

†HULME, WM. (R.I.P.), "Queen's Head" (26721), 15th Lancashire Fusiliers.

HEMSWORTH, GEO., 67, Bolton Road.

HOWARD, ROBT., 14, Hope Street (20522), L.N. Lancs.

HAYDOCK, JEREMIAH, 28, Harold Street (12220), R.A.F.

HILTON, ERNEST, 25, Bolton Road (53815), Lancashire Fusiliers.

HEYES, WM., 5, Scot Lane (61270), 4th Leicesters.

HULME, THOMAS, "Queen's Head" (200284), R.G.A. (121st Battery).

HILTON, ALEX., Railway Street, Hindley (26483), R. Dragoon Guards.

HIGHAM, WM. HY., 618, Bolton Road (65345), Lancashire Fusiliers.

HOLDING, GEO., 35, Bolton Road, H.M.S. "Centurion."

HAYDOCK, JAMES, 96, Scot Lane (67349), 3rd Lancashire Fusiliers.

HAYDOCK, STANLEY, 26, Harold Street (51025), 3rd E. Lancs.

HILL, JOHN, 49, Bolton Road (84972), R.F.A.

HOUGH, ALF., 7, Scot Lane (32190), Durham Light Infantry.

HADDOCK, THOMAS, 98, Withington Lane, R.G.A.

HEYES, THOMAS, 281, Wigan Road (236976), Railway Company.

HOWARTH, ALF., 109, Scot Lane (201000), 1/5th Manchesters.

INGRAM, JOHN, Seddon's Yard (58770), R. Welsh Fusiliers.

†INGRAM, PETER, 77, Scot Lane (P. 15121), M. Foot Police.

ISHERWOOD, HY., 668, Bolton Road (13277), 2nd K.R.R.

IBBETSON, HY., 6, Sunnyside (805232), R.A.F.

IDDON, THOMAS, 456, Bolton Road (82147), Lancashire Fusiliers.

JONES, SIDNEY, 90, Scot Lane (3533), Lancashire Fusiliers.

JOHNSON, HARRY, Lower Walker's Farm, R.A.F.

†JOHNSON, WM. (R.I.P.), 11, Woodfield Street, 1/5th E. Lancs.

JOHNSON, HENRY, 469, Bolton Road, R.F.A.

JACKSON, ALF., 5, Mill Lane (606395), Northumberland Fusiliers.

JONES, SOLOMON, 335, Stanley Road (49420), 83rd Labour Corps.

†JOHNSON, JOHN, Senr. (R.I.P.), 11, Woodfield Street (17754), Royal D. Corps.

JOHNSON, ALBERT, 11, Woodfield Street, 1/5th E. Lancs.

JEPSON, WALT., 12, Harold Street (54042), 4th Lancashire Fusiliers.

JOHNSON, JAMES, 615, Bolton Road (243517), 1/5th L.N. Lancs.

JOHNSON, JOSEPH, £10, Withington Lane (95797), King's Liverpool.

JOHNSON, HENRY, 57, Stanley Road (188672), R.F.A.

JOHNSON, JOHN, 11, Woodfield Street (63947), 43rd Royal Fusiliers.

JONES, JAMES B., 187, Wigan Road (50057), 84th Labour Corps.

KILLOURHY, MICHAEL, 222, Withington Lane (19527), L.N. Lancs.

KAY, JAMES SIMM, 267, Bolton Road (343286), L.N. Lancs.

LEWIS, FRED, 218, Withington Lane (3594), L.N. Lancs.

LEACH, ALBERT, Ashworth Street (20606), Cheshires.

LEIGH, JOHN, 1, Bolton Road, R.F.C.

LEIGH, ROBT. (M.M.), Simm's Square (243069), 1/5th L.N. Lancs.

LANCASTER, WM., Lucas Nook Farm (30737), K.O.S.B.

LANG, THOMAS, Heath Villas, H.M.S.

LORD, JAMES, 4, Bridge Street (13672), R.A.F.

McCOY, PAT. WM., Dicconson Lane, L.N. Lancs.

†MATHER, DONALD (Lieut.) (R.I.P.), Hall Lane.

MERCER, ALEXANDER, 1, Cleveley's Yard (358258), 1/5th Manchesters.

MERCER, ALBERT, 51, Stanley Road (108794), King's Liverpool.

MAKINSON, ALBERT, 608, Bolton Road (18786), Scottish Borderers.

†MONKS, WM. (R.I.P.), 59, Bolton Road, H.M.S. "Warrior."

MITCHELL, JAMES, 3, Mill Lane (O. 89757), Remounts Depot (D. Squad).

MERCER, ERNEST, 38, Bolton Road (41264), R.F.A.

MERCER, JAMES, 38, Bolton Road (363941), A.S.C.

†MEHERS, THOMAS (R.I.P.), 618, Bolton Road (243023), L.N. Lancs.

MEADS, RD., 30, Reservoir Street (75099), R.A.M.C.

MORT, THOMAS, Gerrard Arms (140327), 57th Battery Machine Gun Corps (3rd S.).

MAKINSON, JOHN, 4, Stanley Road (251366), Border Regiment (Lab. Corps).

MERCER, COLIN, 38, Bolton Road (18446), A. Vet. Corps.

MERCER, RD., 38, Bolton Road (251973), Duke of Wellington's.

MONKS, WM., 21, Woodfield Street, H.M.S. "Adamant" (15th Mess).

MILLER, JOSEPH, 44, Scot Lane (20867), 7th Border.

MERCER, HAROLD, 28, Woodfield Street (352018), R.E.

MONKS, JNO. FRANCIS, 10, Duke's Row (354177), R.E.

†MELLING, JAMES (R.I.P.), 66, Scot Lane (23945), L.N. Lancs.

MORT, FRED, Gerrard Arms (331253), 416th Agricultural Company.

MAKINSON, HY., 58, Scot Lane (171243), R.F.A.

MERCER, WM., 20, Scot Lane (K. 50799), H.M.S. "Vivia."

MERCER, ALBERT, 20, Scot Lane, H.M.S.

MERCER, JOHN, 51, Stanley Road (75176), 5th Manchesters.

MERCER, ALBERT, 51, Stanley Road (108794), 3rd K.L.R.

MAKINSON, WRIGHT, 4, Scot Lane (47507), 4th Lancashire Fusiliers.

MOSS, JAMES, 6, Stanley Nook (24484), R.F.A.

NAYLOR, TOM, Birchall Row (3003), K.O.Y.L.I.

NAYLOR, JAMES, 603, Bolton Road (3159), R. Marines (Light Infantry).

PILKINGTON, DAVID, 495, Bolton Road (20521), 3rd L.N. Lancs.

PARR, HORACE, 17, Scot Lane (63327), R.E.

PRESCOTT, HERB., 15, Bolton Road (14961), M. Foot Police.

PILKINGTON, JAMES, 546, Bolton Road (359855), King's Liverpool Scottish.

PENNINGTON, JOHN, Mill Lane (165063), R.G.A.

PILKINGTON, HARRY, 588, Bolton Road (35752), Border Regiment.

PILKINGTON, PERCY, 546, Bolton Road H.M.S. "St. Vincent."

PIMBLETT, SAM., Bradshaw Hall Farm (240433), 5th L.N. Lancs.

PENNING, FRANK LESLIE, 454, Bolton Road (2839), Royal Marines.

PLATT, HAROLD, School Farm, Bagshaw Lane.

PENDLEBURY, ALF., School Close (77791), 3rd Cheshires.

PRESCOTT, ROBT., 3, Hindley Mill Cottage (24349), R.F.A.

PIMBLEY, PETER, 20, Woodfield Street (398813), 699th Agricultural Company.

ROYLE, JAMES, Reservoir Street (16818), Border Regiment.

ROTHERHAM, JAMES, 10, Bolton Road (74632), R.F.A.

RIGBY, ALF., 45, Bolton Road (109665), Tank Corps.

RUTTER, JOHN, 2, School Close (352421), R.E.

RIGBY, GEORGE, 61, Stanley Road (41748), Labour Company.

ROTHERAM, WM. VICTOR, 10, Bolton Road (109604), 3rd King's Liverpool.

RATCLIFFE, WILFRED, 11, Harold Street, H.M.S. "Early."

ROSBOTHAM, JOSEPH, 234, Withington Lane (458237), Labour Company.

RATCLIFFE, LEVI, Stanley Road (148794), R.G.A.

RUDGE, LEONARD, 132, Withington Lane, H.M.S. (Depot Ships).

†SIMM, WM. (R.I.P.), 304, Heyes' Square (17261), L.N. Lancs.

SEDDON, WALTER H., 58, Bolton Road (882244), R.H.A.

SOUTHERN, ALB., 3, Harold Street (80313), R.F.A.

SALT, FRED, 171, Wigan Road (7645), 2nd South Lancs.

SALT, JESSE, 171, Wigan Road (8107), 1/5th Manchesters (W. Riding).

†SALT, ERNEST (R.I.P.), 171, Wigan Road (1982), 4th South Lancs.

†SUMNER, RD. KELLETT (R.I.P.), Withington Lane, 1/5th Manchesters.

†SMITH, THOMAS (R.I.P.), 1, Black Horse Square (36057), 10th Lancashire Fus.

SIMM, JOHN, Ephraim's Fold, 9th E. Yks.

STOREY, JONATHAN, 214, Withington Lane (203394), 1/10th Manchesters.

†SOUTHAM, WM. (R.I.P.), 18, Hope Street (11410), 3rd York and Lancaster.

SIMM, ALEX., Simm's Square (77879), 15th Durham Light Infantry.

SIMM, GEO., Withington Lane, 5th M'rs.

SMAIL, ALEX., 581, Bolton Road, York and Lancaster.

SOUTHERN, WALT., Ephraim's Fold (201088), 5th Manchesters.

SEDDON, PERCY, 11, Leigh Street (36489), Lancashire Fusiliers.

SEDDON, THOMAS, 540, Bolton Road (76017), R.A.M.C.

STICKLE, EDWARD.

SMITH, WM., 1, Heaton Street (201487), 1/5th Manchesters.

SOUTHERN, GEO., Harold Street (4267), 5th Manchesters.

SCOTT, WM., Ainscough's Farm, Grenadier Guards.

SOUTHERN, JAMES, 5, Pennington Green (71735), R.G.A.

SMITH, DAVID, 1, Black Horse Square (200553), 251st Labour Company.

SIMM, JAMES, 37, Woodfield Street (M/2 178262), 65th A.A.C. Sec. M.B., M.T.

SIMM, JOHN ALEX. POWELL, 37, Woodfield Street (61707), 78th R.E.

SOUTHWORTH, ROBT., Bolton Road (387596), 25th King's Liverpool.

STEELE, EDWARD, 14, Harold Street (40422), 15th Cheshires.

SMITH, HENRY, 1, Heaton Street (40479), L.N. Lancs.

SUMNER, JOHN, Withington Lane.

SEDDON, ANDREW, 540, Bolton Road (333047), R.E.

SIMM, THOMAS, 467, Bolton Road (109199), King's Liverpool.

SEDDON, RICHARD, 26, Scot Lane (67457), 3rd Lancashire Fusiliers.

SEDDON, JAMES HOPE, Wales, H.M.S.

SUTTON, SYLVESTER, 2, Sumner Street (132464), R.F.A.

SILCOCK, ROBT., 148, Withington Lane (260219), R.F.A.

SEDDON, DAVID, 540, Bolton Road (41985), Hampshires.

SOUTHWORTH, ROB, 7, Pennington Green (39579), Lancashire Fusiliers.

TAYLOR, WM., 278, Withington Lane, 5th Manchesters.

TARBUCK, WM., Withington Lane, 2/5th Manchesters.

TAYLOR, SAMUEL, Latham's Farm, Hall Lane (131473), R.G.A.

TAYLOR, HAROLD, Hindley, H.M.S. "Ben More."

THOMPSON, HAROLD, 40, Scot Lane, H.M.S. "Dauntless."

TAYLOR, HORACE, 1, School Close (108697), 1st King's Liverpool.

THOMPSON, JAMES, 40, Scot Lane (64910), 1/7th Lancashire Fusiliers.

TROUGHTON, CHRIS., 9, School Close (165485), R.G.A.

VALENTINE, WM., 1, Scot Lane (184606), R.F.A.

WINNARD, FRED, 4, School Close (9263), H.M.S. "Blackburn."

WRIGHT, WM., Withington Lane, 5th L.N. Lancs.

WHITTLE, JOSEPH, Cleveley's Yard, L.N. Lancs.

WALKDEN, REUBEN, Ashworth Street, R.F.A.

WALKER, ROBERT, Landlord's Farm (40092), Rifle Battalion (N.Z.).

WATMOUGH, FRANK, 108, Bolton Road.

WALKER, JAMES, 262, Bolton Road (191092), Machine Gun Corps.

WALKER, ERNEST, Ashcroft Street (R. 13280), K.R.R.

WALKER, ISAAC, 544, Bolton Road (57321), R.G.A.

†WALKER, JOHN (R.I.P.), Landlord's Farm (Z/1165), 10th Mounted Rifles (N.Z.).

WILKINSON, JOHN, 37, Bolton Road (137839), R.F.A.

WALLIS, EDGAR M., Aspull Firs, N.Z. (F.A.).

†WALLIS, HUBERT J. (R.I.P.), Aspull Firs (17634), Royal Warwick.

WINNARD, RALPH, Near Malt Kiln (60641), 26th Div. Cycling Company.

WINNARD, ELI, Near Malt Kiln (34351), R.H.A. (Y Battery).

WESTBY, ARTHUR, 121, Dicconson Lane (343269), R.A.F.

WALKER, THOMAS, 262, Bolton Road (260690), R.F.A. (4th Brigade).

WINROW, JOHN, 147, Wigan Road (109101), K.L.R. (B Company).

WALLS, WM., 7, Bolton Road, H.M.S. "Spear."

WALLS, JAMES, 18, Bolton Road (2954), H.M.S. "Albemarle."

WILSON, J. W., 151, Wigan Road (65065), Lancashire Fusiliers.

WILSON, THOMAS, 151, Wigan Road, Cadet Corps (Rhyl).

WHEELER, CHAS., 9, Simm's Square (110924), Royal Fusiliers.

YOUNG, JNO. EDWARD, 62, Scot Lane (20403), Highland L. Infantry (Missing).

YOUNG, JOSEPH, 62, Scot Lane (37054), 6th L.N. Lancs.

APPENDIX 3
Extract from Kelly's Directory 1924

ASPULL with HAIGH and PENNINGTON GREEN.

ASPULL is a township and village in the parish of Wigan and together with Haigh was formed into a parish April 3, 1838, and is on the Union canal from Liverpool to Hull, 2½ miles north-east from Wigan railway station, 16 west-by-north from Manchester, in the Westhoughton division of the county, hundred of Salford, petty sessional division, union, county court district and rural deanery of Wigan and archdeaconry and diocese of Liverpool. Aspull township was governed by a Local Board, formed in 1876, but under the Local Government Act, 1894, it is now governed by an Urban District Council. The church of St. John the Baptist, at New Springs, a chapel of ease to St. David's, Haigh, erected in 1897, is a structure of red brick in the Gothic style, consisting of chancel, nave and a north-west porch, and will seat 550 persons. The register dates from 1873. There are two Roman Catholic churches, erected in 1858, and dedicated to Our Lady of the Immaculate Conception, and the Holy Family, and there are also Wesleyan Methodist, Independent Methodist and Primitive Methodist chapels. The Wigan Coal and Iron Co. Limited have very extensive and valuable coal and cannel mines in this township; there are also large malt kilns and a cotton mill. The Urban District Council, who are lords of the manor, John Hodges esq. and Roger Leigh esq. are the chief land-owners. The soil is clayey; subsoil, stiff clay. The chief crops are wheat, oats and potatoes. The area is 1,906 acres, of which 23 are water; rateable value, £19,506; the population of the civil township and Urban District in 1921 was 7,851 and of the ecclesiastical parish in 1911, 3,978. The population of the wards in 1921 was: East, 2,298; New Springs, 3,167 and North, 2,386.

Railway Stations, Dicconson Lane & Aspull, William Grimshaw, station master

HAIGH is a township and village on the Leeds and Liverpool canal, and together with Aspull was formed into an ecclesiastical parish April 3, 1856; it is 2 miles north-west from Red Rock station, in the Chorley division of the county and the hundred of West Derby. The church of St. David, a plain building of stone in the Early English style, erected in 1833 and enlarged in 1886, consists of chancel, nave, north porch, vestries, organ chamber, baptistery and a western turret containing one bell: the interior has been re-seated and a new organ erected as a memorial to Jacob Wilson Fair esq. J.P.: there are seven stained windows: the baptistery was rebuilt in 1916 at the expense of the Rev. C. H. James M.A. (vicar) and his wife, in memory of their four soldier sons: the baptistery is panelled in light carved oak, and has an Italian mosaic floor and a ceiling decorated in gold, blue and red: the church affords 640 sittings. The register dates from the year 1833. The living is a vicarage, net yearly value £360, with residence, in the gift of the rector of Wigan, and held since 1921 by the Rev. Edwyn Lisle Marsden, hon. C.F. The Receptacle, founded by Dame Dorothy Bradshaigh in 1774, consists of five houses for the use of ten poor persons, male and female; the interest on the fund in the hands of the Charity Commissioners amounts to about £152 yearly; each pensioner is allowed £4 yearly and a further sum of 10s. on Christmas Day, besides coals and medical attendance. There are valuable mines of coal, belonging to the Wigan Coal and Iron Co. Limited, and an extensive brewery belonging to Messrs. John Sumner and Co. Haigh Hall, situated in a splendid park of 500 acres, is the beautiful seat of the Earl of Crawford and Balcarres K.T., P.C. who is lord of the manor and sole owner of the township. The Hall was formerly the residence of the Bradshaw or Bradshaigh family, baronets of Haigh; it contains a fine library of over 100,000 volumes, chiefly collected by the late earl, including many rare and choice works; the mansion, being on a lofty eminence, commands extensive prospects over thirteen counties and is surrounded by a well-wooded park. The soil is clay; the subsoil is stiff clay. The chief crops are wheat, oats and potatoes. The area is 2,130 acres, of which 68 are water; rateable value, £13,282; the population in 1921 was 953 in the township; that of the ecclesiastical parish in 1911 was 5,386.

Parish Clerk, John Casson.

PUBLIC ELEMENTARY SCHOOLS.

Mixed, with master's house, built in about 1846, for 300 children; John Ackers Wood, master

Red Rock (mixed), built in 1871, for 115 children; Miss Margaret Watmough, mistress

RAILWAY STATION.

Red Rock, William A. Glenister, station master

PENNINGTON GREEN is in the township of Aspull, and in 1883 was formed into an ecclesiastical parish from the parish of Haigh and Aspull, under the name of Aspull St. Elizabeth's. The church of St. Elizabeth of Hungary, erected in 1878-80, chiefly at the expense of Roger Leigh esq. is a building of brick, mainly in the Gothic style, and consists of chancel, nave, south aisle, south-west porch and a turret containing one bell: there are 420 sittings. The register dates from the year 1881. The living is a vicarage, net yearly value £272, in the gift of trustees, and held since 1912 by the Rev. Frederic Cyril Wallis M.A. of Clare College, Cambridge, who resides at The Firs. The population of the ecclesiastical parish in 1911 was 3,978.

Haigh.1926.
Haigh Brewery chimney, St. David's Church and Haigh Windmill are all visible on the sky line.

Post, M. O. & T. Office, 33 Wigan road, New Springs, Richard Leonard Turner, sub-postmaster; letters through Wigan.
Post & M. O. Office, 3 Scot lane, Aspull, James Heyes, sub-postmaster. Post & M. O. Office, Withington lane, New Springs, James Green, sub-postmaster. Post, M. O. & T. Office, 26 Haigh road, Aspull, John Casson, sub-postmaster.
Post & M. O. Office, 585 Bolton road, Aspull, William Hope, sub-postmaster

ASPULL URBAN DISTRICT COUNCIL.

Offices, White hall.

Meeting day, 1st wednesday in month.

Members.

Chairman, Edward Rigby.
Vice-Chairman, William Sword.

Retire April, 1924.

| Thomas Heyes | Enoch Lively |
| Robert Johnson | |

Retire April, 1925.

| James Heyes | John Hope |
| Thomas Heyes | |

Retire April, 1926.

| John W. Armstrong | Edward Rigby |
| William Bird | William Sword |

Officers.

Clerk & Collector, Richard Armour, Crawford villas
Treasurer, David Goldsworth, banker, Wigan
Medical Officer of Health, Luther Cooke L.R.C.P. & S. Edin. Haigh road, Aspull
Engineers, George Heaton & Sons, King street, Wigan
Sanitary Inspector & Surveyor, James Occleshaw, Queen's Head hotel, Aspull
County Police Station, David Millar, sergeant

PUBLIC ELEMENTARY SCHOOLS.

Bolton road (mixed), built in 1868, for 300 children; John Gordon, master; Miss Morris, infants' mistress
St. John the Baptist, New Springs (mixed), built in the year 1872 by the late Earl of Crawford for 446 children, together with houses for the master & mistress; Harold Fairhurst, master
St. Elizabeth's (mixed), Bolton road, built in 1878 by Roger Leigh esq. for 191 children; Mrs. E. Strowger, mistress
Roman Catholic (mixed), Cale lane, built in 1887, for 242 children; Mrs. Maud Entwistle, mistress
Roman Catholic (mixed), Haigh road, built in 1864, for 240 children; Miss Florence Moore, mistress
Wesleyan (mixed), School Close, built in 1879, & enlarged in 1899, for 322 children; William Layland, master; Miss Emma Eckersley, infants' mistress

ASPULL.

Cooke Luther, Ashfield, Haigh road
Egbers Rev. Henry (Roman Catholic), Haigh road
Mather Charles, Merehurst, Hall lane
Rawcliffe Miss, Culraven
Sword William, Moorland house
Topping Jn. 137 Wigan rd. New Springs
Wallis Rev. Frederic Cyril M.A. (vicar of St. Elizabeth of Hungary), The Firs, Pennington green

COMMERCIAL.

Alker Thomas, blacksmith, Hornby's row
Armour Richard, clerk & collector to the Urban District Council, Whitehall & registrar of births & deaths, Crawford villas
Ashton Elizabeth (Mrs.), farmer, Bolton rd
Atherton & Johnson, grocers, 107 Wigan road, New Springs
Atherton John Wm. shopkpr. 45 Bolton rd
Bailey John, Dog & Partridge P.H. Wigan road
Balfour George, farmer, Stanley Nook frm
Balfour Stephen, boot maker, 100 Haigh rd
Banks Edward, Royal P.H. 1 Chapel st
Beasley Fras. J. beer retlr. 15 Wigan road
Beeston Elizabeth Ann (Mrs.), shopkeeper, 77 Wigan road
Bell & Sons, painters, 71 Wigan road, New Springs
Bimson Ebenezer, beer retailer, 104 Wigan road, New Springs
Birchall Martha (Mrs.), shopkeeper, 93 Wigan road
Boardman Wm. beer retlr. 15 & 17 Cale la
Booth John, grocer, 175 Wigan road, New Springs
Broadhurst John William, grocer, 125 Wigan road, New Springs
Bula Spinning Co. (1920) Ltd. cotton spnnrs
Cartwright Jas. beer retlr. Hornby's row
Causey Mary Ann (Mrs.), farmer
Charnock Thomas, Gerrard's Arms, 615 Bolton road
Chisnall John, shopkeeper, 35 Scot lane
Christopher John, grocer, 99 & 101 Wigan road, New Springs
Collier John & Mary (Miss), farmers, Manor House farm
Conservative Club (William Collier, sec)
Cooke Luther L.R.C.P. & S. surgeon & medical officer of health to the Urban District Council, Ashfield, Haigh road & farmer, Holly Nook farm
Cox Thomas, farmer, Ratcliffe road
Croston Richard, greengrocer, 67 Wigan rd
Dempsey Catherine (Mrs.), Ivy P.H. New Springs
Dolan Alex. hair dresser, 105 Wigan rd. New Springs
Eastman Robert, wringing machine repairer, 16 Crown street, New Springs
Ekersley Paul, shopkpr. 22 Ratcliffe road
Fairclough Edward, draper, 34 Wigan rd
Farrar James, beer retailer, Stanley road
Farrimond Henry, fried fish dealer, 7 Wigan road, New Springs
Farrimond Thos. H. shopkpr. 8 Ratcliffe rd
Fielding John, clogger, 41 Scot lane
Fielding Saml. shopkeeper, 42 Scot lane
Gerrard Walter, shopkeeper, 79 Wigan rd
Gormally Thos. Commercial P.H. 139 Cale la
Green Elizabeth (Mrs.), midwife, 133 Withington lane
Green James, clogger & sub-postmaster, 137 Withington lane, Top Lock
Green Jonathan William, confectioner 83, & clogger 85, Wigan rd. New Springs
Griffiths John, farmer, Gidlow Hall farm

Haddock Bros. coal mers. Withington la
Hallam Benjamin, boot & shoe maker, 73 Wigan road, New Springs
Halliday & Constantine Ltd. cotton goods manufacturers, Dicconson mill
Halliwell Alice M. (Mrs.), Kirkless Hall P.H. Top Lock
Hampson Richard, beer retlr. 39 Bolton rd
Hardman Henry, fried fish dealer, 69 Wigan road, New Springs
Harrington Emma (Mrs.), shopkeeper, 173 Wigan road
Harrington John, Running Horses P.H. Smithy road
Harrison Joseph, butcher, 1 Wigan road
Harrison Robert, beer retailer, 179 Withington lane, Top Lock
Harvey Julia (Mrs.), shopkpr. 96 Cale la
Hayes James, shopkeeper, 3 Scot lane
Hayes William, shopkeeper, 47 Wigan rd
Hewitt Sarah Jane (Mrs.), shopkeeper, 7 Chapel street
Heyes Ezekiah, grocer, 48 Scot lane
Heyes Joseph, beer retailer, Ratcliffe road
Heyes Thomas, bricklayer, 35 Wigan road
Highton William, butcher, 103 Wigan rd
Hill James, shopkeeper, 154 Withington lane, Top Lock
Hilton Thos. farmer, Walker's Higher frm
Hindley Elizh. (Mrs.), frmr. Penningtn.grn
Holcroft Henry, farmer
Holcroft Robert, farmer, Walker's farm
Holding Fanny (Mrs.), shopkeeper, 113 Wigan road
Hope Jas. Southern, beer ret. 482 Bolton rd
Hope John, shopkeeper, 574 Bolton rd
Hope William, grocer, & sub-post office 585 Bolton road
Hough Robert, beer retailer, 617 Bolton rd
Humphreys John William, Queen's Head P.H. Wigan road
Jackson William, shopkeeper, 3 Wigan road, New Springs
Johnson Henry, farmer, Bradley's farm
Johnson Hy. farmer, Lower Walker's frm
Johnson Herbert, butcher, Haigh road
Johnson Robert, shopkeeper, 47 Haigh rd
Kirkby John Alfred, caretaker Liverpool Waterworks, Reservoir house
Knight Charles, shopkeeper, 130 Wigan rd
Labour Club (William Armstrong, sec.), New Springs
Lee Arthur, shopkeeper, 81 Wigan road, New Springs
Leigh James, farmer, Bolton road
Lockhart Wm. shopkeeper, 210 Withington lane, Top Lock
Lucas John, grocer, 470 Bolton road
Marsden George, farmer, Stanley Nook & Hilton farms
Melling Thomas, beer retailer, Bark hill, New Springs
Miller Elizh. (Miss), shopkpr. 161 Wigan rd
Miller William, farmer, Bark Hill farm
Mobs William, grocer, Stanley road
Molyneux William, pawnbroker, 25 Wigan road, New Springs
Moore John, butcher, 13a. Wigan road
Moore Joseph, Red Lion P.H. Haigh road
Morris Elizh. (Mrs.), beer ret. 38 Ratcliffe rd
Moss James, beer retailer, 72 Scot lane
Occleshaw James, sanitary inspector to the Urban District Council, Queen's Head hotel
Owens John, beer retailer, 50 Haigh road
Orrell John W. boot repr. 2 Wigan road
Parsons Tom, shopkeeper, 77 Leeds road, Top Lock
Pass Thomas, fried fish dealer, 144 Withington lane
Pearson Henry, farmer, Top Bank

Pendlebury John Roger, farmer, Higher Highfield farm & Gorses farm
Pennington John, farmer, Rodger's farm
Pilkington Wm. clogger, 565 Bolton road
Pimblett William, farmer, Bagshaw lane
Powell Mary (Miss), shopkpr. 36 Wigan rd
Ratcliffe John, farmer, Marsh farm
Richardson Peter, fishmngr. 149 Wigan rd
Rigby Alfred, grocer, 45 Bolton road
Rigby Edward, Free Trade inn, 13 Wigan rd
Robinson Thomas, shopkeeper, 43 Scot la
Rose Cecilia (Mrs.), shopkeeper, 28 Wigan road, New Springs
Rowland & Clarke, grocers, 60 Wigan rd
Rowson Arthur, Crown hotel, Wigan road, New Springs
Rushton Harvey, farmer, Shaw's feld
Rushton O. & G. Limited, 561 Bolton rd.; 87 Wigan road & Dicconson lane
Saxon Thomas, greengrocer, 63 Wigan rd
Shepherd John, shopkeeper, 11 Stanley rd
Sheppard Alex. shopkpr. 276 Wigan road
Sheppard John, beer retailer, Scot lane
Sheppard William, New inn, Ratcliffe rd
Smalley Ann (Miss), draper, 97 Wigan rd. New Springs
Southall William, shopkecpr. 110 Wigan la
Sumner Richard, beer retlr. 55 Wigan rd
Tattersall Wm. shopkeeper, 119 Wigan rd
Taylor John, fried fish dealer, 115 Wigan road, New Springs
Tetsill Thomas, draper, 53 Wigan road
Townley Harry, shopkeeper, Dicconson la
Turner Fred J. butcher, 65 Wigan road
Turner Richard Leonard, stationer, & post office, 33 Wigan rd. New Springs
Valentine Brothers, farmers, Bradshaw Hall farm
Whitfield Elizh. (Mrs.), shopkpr. 29 Wigan rd
Wigan Coal & Iron Co. Ltd. (John F. Gillott, manager; Sir Thomas R. Ratcliffe-Ellis. sec.), coal proprietors; registered office, Kirkless; Wigan office, 51 Wallgate
Wigan & District Equitable Co-operative Society Limited (branches), 19 & 21 Bolton road & 32 Chapel st. New Springs
Wilkinson John, carter, Bolton road
Wilson John, beer retailer, 3 Bark hill
Wilson Robert, fried fish dlr. 80 Scot la
Wyatt George, shopkeeper, Leeds street
Yates Arthur, shopkeeper, 19 Wigan road, New Springs
Yates Mary A. (Mrs.), shopkeeper, 23 Wigan road
Young Joseph, shopkeeper, 64 Scot lane

HAIGH.

PRIVATE RESIDENTS.

Crawford & Balcarres The Earl of K.T., P.C., D.L. Haigh hall: & 7 Audley sq W 1 & Carlton & Burlington Fine Arts clubs, London
Brown William, Prospect house
Burgess Charles, Douglas vale
Christopher Richard, Holly bank
Dunn Arthur, Curfew house
Eastham Thomas, Holly Bank house
Fair Arthur Edward J.P. Haighlands
Gillott Joseph F. Moat house
Gregory John, Whittle Tag farm
Hampson Ernest T. Douglas cottage
Hewlett Alfred, Haigh cottage
McCutcheon William, Winstanley's farm
Marsden Rev. Edwyn Lisle hon. C.F. (vicar of St. David's), The Vicarage
Martindale Mrs. Standish view
Simpson Charles C. W. Longhurst
Spencer Peter, Sea view
Thompson George O. Haigh house
Watmough Miss M. School ho. Red Rock

HAIGH

COMMERCIAL.

Bargh John, farm bailiff to the Earl of Crawford & Balcarres K.T., P.C., D.L. Home farm
Blackburn Thos. farmr. Brock Mill farm
Boyd William, head gardener to the Earl of Crawford & Balcarres K.T., P.C., D.L.
Casson John, grocer, & post office
Cliffe William, farmer, Patchcroft farm
Cooper Jane (Mrs.), farmer, Fir Tree frm
Ireland Thomas H. clerk of the works to the Earl of Crawford & Balcarres K.T., P.C., D.L
Fair Arthur Edward J.P. estate agent to the Earl of Crawford & Balcarres K.T., P.C., D.L. T N Haigh 4
Gibson George (Mrs.), Crawford Arms P.H

Gregory Elisha, shopkeeper, 28 Haigh rd
Haigh Dyeing Co. Limited, dyers, Brock mill. T N 183 Wigan
Halton J. J. farmer, Tucker's Hill farm
Harrimond M. (Miss), district nurse
Hodge Charles, farmer, Red Rock & Worthington farms
Hodge Mary E. & Ann (Misses), shopkeepers, Red Rock
Jeffreys, Miller & Co. Ltd. malt extract manufacturers, Leyland mill
Johnson Herbert, farmer, Lane ends
Marshall Stanley, farmer, Leyland Mill frm
Marshall Thomas, farmer, Lower House & Park House farms
Mawdsley Ellen (Mrs.), frmr. Willowby frm

Mort John, farmer, Marsh's farm
Murray James, farmer, Freezeland farm
Rhoden Thomas S. & Bunnell George, farmers, Waterworks farm
Southern Mary E. (Mrs.), Balcarres Arms P.H
Strange James, farrier, Nightingale farm
Sumner John & Co. brewers, Haigh brewery. T N Haigh 2
Taylor Francis, farmer, Astley's farm
Thorpe Edmond, farmer, Toddington farm
Walker William, farmer, Pennington farm
Whittle Richard, blacksmith
Wigan Golf Club (John Prescott, treasurer)
Wigan Motor Bodies Limited, motor body makers, Mariebonne works

ABOUT ASPULL - A REPRISE

BRINSOP STREET ASPULL

Residents of Brinsop Street, Aspull, celebrating the Coronation of King George VI and Queen Elizabeth. 1937

BOLTON ROAD ASPULL

Right: Shallicker's Fish &Chip Shop, Bolton Road, Aspull. Circa 1950.*(left to right)* Seated are Sam Heyes, Cyril Westhead, Richard Thompson and Barry Smith. The small boy has not been identified.

Below left: In the doorway of No 616 Bolton Road, Aspull are *(left to right)* Jane Ann Bond(snr), Lily Bond (with dog) and Jane Ann Bond (jnr). 1930.

Bellow Right: Outside No 618, Bolton Road , Aspull. 1936. Present are *(left to right)* Wilfred Westhead, Harold Bond, Jim Bond (back), Jack Westhead (seated) Thomas Chamberlain and Jack Westhead (snr).

BOLTON ROAD ASPULL

Pictured outside No 618 Bolton Road, Aspull, are *(left to right back row:)* Thomas Chamberlain, Jim Bond and Richard Bond. *(.left to right front row:)* Margaret Smith, Irene Smith, Mrs J Bond and Mrs Jane Ann Smith.

Dicconson Mill Bridge, Aspull. 1957. Alan Lord *(left)* and Thomas Chamberlain

Bolton Road, Aspull. Circa 1938. On the left is William Thompson, with Leonard Westhead, Jack and Lily Bond at the door of No 616

Thomas Chamberlain (left) and Nat Chapman at the entrance to Borsdane Wood. 1926.

V.E. Day celebrations on the mill field off Leigh Street, Aspull. 1945 (May8th).Standing on the extreme left, with headscarf is Myra Freeman.

Aspull youths in Borsdane Woods. Circa 1938. *(left to right back row:)* James Hyland, Ernest Heyes, David Thompson, Wifred Westhead. *(.left to right front row:)* Johnnie Brook's & Charles Halliwell

MILL LANE, ASPULL

Father and son, both Thomas Chamberlain, in Mill Lane. 1936

Lily and John Holden with Thomas Chamberlain 1946.

(From left to right) John Holden, Thomas Chamberlain, Ethel Chapman, Nat Chapman and Annie Chapman. 1946

WORRELL'S YARD

Worrell's yard, Aspull. 1937. The Bond family outside their home. Harold Bond can be seen in the uniform of Hindley Prize Band.

(From left to right) Annie Chapman, John Holden, Lily Holden, Raymond Bond, and Leonard Westhead.

ST MARGARET'S CHURCH, PENNINGTON GREEN

Demolition of the Church.

Ince Old Hall from an engraving by N.G. Philips, published in 1822.

"The manor of Ince, in the parish of Wigan, of which the Hall of Ince, or Ince Old Hall, was the capital messuage, was anciently held under the Barons of Newton in Mackerfield, by a family bearing the local name, (i.e. de Ince), who also held the neighbouring Manor of Aspull under the Barons of Manchester".

From 'Views of the Old Halls of Lancashire and Cheshire' written by Hon. and Rev. Canon G.T.O. Bridgeman, M.A. Published by Henry Gray, London. 1893.

Dicconson Mill Football Team 1911.
The Mill is visible far left. Amongst the team are J. Webber, Sam Westhead, Jim Bond, W. Brooks, Richard Bond and Roland Heyes.

Bolton Road, Aspull. 1958.
Photograph taken during the Aspull Carnival.
Shallicker's Fish & Chip Shop is in the background
Hugh Hayes is second from the left at the front.

Edward Bond and Colin Heyes in Borsdane Wood. 1910.

Colin Heyes in the Aspull Carnival dressed as the fighting Parson! 1958.

Pictured from the left are T. Lythgoe, Barry Smith, J. Hope and Irene Smith Brinsop Street, Aspull. 1946.

Harold Crompton Pictured in Hope Street, Aspull.

Belgians Residing At Hindley Hall, Hindley.

Belgian Refugees at Hindley Hall during the First World War.

THE ROYAL VISIT TO WIGAN
(JUNE, 1873).

HAVIN' a bit o' leighshure toime,
  Aw'll just sit deawn an' pen a rhoime,
Abeawt that greight hospishus day
Which Wiggin shortly will display.

On th' third o' June aw understand,
Th' owd burro' will bi deckd' quoite grand,
An nowt bud reet, for on that day,
A Royal pair will visit Haigh.

Wheer eawr respected Earl, aw know,
Will on their Highnesses bestow,
Thoose good things money con procure,
To mak' their happiness secure.

Yo' should see th' vast preparashuns,
Up ud th' Ho an' throo th' plantashuns ;
Besides the noble House o' Haigh,
Will feast some hundreds on thad day.

Leds cheer booath Lord an' Lady C.,
For helpin' on th' Infirmary ;
Their koindly akshuns, awve no deawt,
Hav' browt this grand event abeawt.

Becose, wi me yo'll o agree,   .
Thad they invoited Royalty,
Afther th' Wiggin Corporashun
Had sent up their depitashun.

Awm shure eawr wealthy worthy Mayor *
Every good thing will prepare,
For th' Royal guests, an' th' rest o'th' bunch,
Thad he intends axin to lunch.

His spred ull boath bi rich an' grand,
Becose he's money at command ;
Aw'll bet a shillin' to a groat
He's cash enough to sink a boat.

Awm gradely glad thad Mesther Simm
Eawr able chief, ull dine wi him ;
His wurship's very koind indeed,
For thus invitin' him to feed.

Moi word, ther'll be a bonny stur,
Foak lookin' eawt ud every dur ;
Greight multytudes ull sheawt an' sing
For th' Prince o' Wales, eawr futer King.

May He who guvverns up abuv,
Breathe on the Royal pair His luv,
An' send th' owd sun to shed his rays,
Throoeawt eawr land on thoose three days.

* N. Eckersley, Esq., J.P.

Iv we're bless'd wi pleasant weather,
Led us o' unoite together,
An' thank th' Creater uv eawr frame,
For koindly sendin' us the same.

So, neaw, aw'll bid yo o' adew,
Aw think awve written loines enoo,
An' afther th' busy stur is o'er,
Iv awve spare toime, aw'll tell yo more.

Poem by James Brown from Haigh

Books by the same author:-

About Horwich	ISBN No.0950877271*
Rivington, Lancashire	" 0 95087728X*
Adlington & District, Lancashire	" 0 1873500017*
About Blackrod	" 1 873500025
Old Rivington & District	" 0 952618710
Horwich Locomotive Works	" 0 952618729
A Short History of Heath Charnock Isolation Hospital.	
Leverhulme's Rivington...	" 0 952618737
More About Horwich	" 0 952618745

* Currently out of print